SUPER QUICK
COLORFUL
QUILTS

SUPER QUICK
COLORFUL
QUILTS

edited by

Rosemary Wilkinson

Good Books

Intercourse, PA 17534
800/762-7171
www.goodbks.com

First published in North America by Good Books (2004),
Intercourse, PA 17534 • 800/762-7171 • www.goodbks.com

Text, photography and illustrations © 2004 New Holland Publishers (UK) Ltd
Quilt designs copyright © Sharon Chambers, Nikki Foley, Katharine Guerrier, Jean Hunt, Gail Smith,
Sarah Wellfair, Rita Whitehorn, Alison Wood, Dorothy Wood

Copyright © 2004 New Holland Publishers (UK) Ltd

SUPER QUICK COLORFUL QUILTS
Good Books, Intercourse, PA 17534
International Standard Book Number: 1-56148-465-2

Editor: Rosemary Wilkinson
Design: Frances de Rees
Photographs: Shona Wood
Illustrations: Carrie Hill
Template diagrams: Kuo Kang Chen

Reproduction by Pica Digital PTE Ltd, Singapore
Printed and bound in Malaysia by
Times Offset (M) Sdn Bhd

NOTE
The measurements for each project are given in imperial and metric. Use only one set of measurements
– do not interchange them because they are not direct equivalents.

CIP data available on request

CONTENTS

Techniques and Tips

The twenty patchwork quilts in this new collection are designed for beginners and those whose time is limited. Although they use just three shapes, the square, the rectangle and the triangle, they still show an amazing variety of designs, made all the more exciting by a clever choice of fabrics in three main groups of colorways: bright, primary and pastel. These shapes are cut quickly using the rotary cutter rather than with a template, and they are machine stitched together with chain-piecing wherever possible. The quilt "sandwich" (of backing fabric, batting and the pieced top) is held together with machine quilting, big stitch hand quilting or with simple ties and buttons. Two methods are used for the binding – one using four strips applied separately to the four sides, producing abutted corners, and the other, slightly more complicated, using a continuous binding, mitered at the corners. Simple appliqué is introduced using a heart template and a technique called slashing. Chenille is used as an alternative to piecing to produce a highly textured surface for a really cuddly quilt.

MATERIALS

PATCHWORK FABRICS

The easiest fabrics to work with for patchwork are closely woven, 100% cotton. They "cling" together, making a stable unit for cutting and stitching, they don't fray too readily and they press well. Quilting shops and suppliers stock a fantastic range in both solid colors and prints, usually in 45 in/115 cm widths, and most of the quilts in this book are based on these cottons.

For each of the quilts featured, there are four alternative colorways, showing the many different effects that can be achieved with each pattern. Fabric designers bring out new ranges all the time, and a quick and effective way of choosing fabrics for a quilt is to use the different colorways within one design or different designs in the same colors.

BACKING AND BINDING FABRICS

The backing fabric should be the same type and weight as the fabrics used in the patchwork top. It can be a coordinating color or it can be a strong contrast. You can also be adventurous and piece the backing, too, to make a reversible quilt. In either case, the color of the binding needs to work with both the top and the backing fabric design.

BATTING

Various types of batting are available in cotton, polyester, wool or mixed fibers. They can be bought in pre-cut sizes suitable for cot quilts and different sizes of bed quilts or in specific lengths cut from a bolt. They also come in different weights or "lofts" depending on how padded you want the quilt to be. Lightweight polyester batting is the most commonly used, but some are more suited to hand quilting. Some need to be closely quilted to prevent them from bunching up; others can be quilted up to 8 in/20 cm apart. Follow the manufacturer's instructions if in doubt.

QUANTITIES

The quantities given at the beginning of each project have been calculated to allow for a bit extra – just in case! The various pieces cut for each quilt use the rotary cutting method and, unless otherwise stated, are cut from across the width of the fabric.

A few of the quilts combine cutting down the length of the fabric with cutting across the width. This is to make the most economical use of fabric or to obtain border pieces cut in one piece.

Unless otherwise stated, any ¼ yard/25 cm requirement is the "long" quarter – the full width of the fabric – and not the "fat" quarter which is a piece 18 x 22 in/50 x 56 cm.

PREPARATION

All fabrics should be washed prior to use in order to wash out any excess dye and to avoid fabrics shrinking at different rates. Wash each fabric separately and rinse – repeatedly if necessary - until the water is clear of any color run. (If washing in a machine, cut a piece of white fabric from a larger piece. Place one piece in with the wash. After the wash, compare the white fabric with its other half. If they are the same, the fabric did not run. If a particular fabric continues to color the water no matter how many times it is washed/rinsed and you have your heart set on using it, try washing it together with a small piece of each of the fabrics you intend to use with it. If these fabrics retain their original color, i.e. they match the pieces not washed with the offending fabric, you would probably be safe in using it. But if in doubt – don't!

Once washed, and before they are completely dry, iron the fabrics and fold them selvage to selvage – as they were originally on the bolt – in preparation for cutting. Be sure to fold them straight so that the selvages line up evenly, even if the cut edges are not parallel (this will be fixed later).

THREADS

For machine quilting use lightweight or monofilament threads. For quilting by hand, use a thread labeled "quilting thread" which is heavier than normal sewing thread. There are several manufacturers of this thread, and it comes in many different colors. Some threads are 100% cotton; others have a polyester core that is wrapped with cotton. You can use a thread either to match or to contrast with the fabric that is being quilted. It is also acceptable to use several colors on the same piece of work. If the quilt is to be tied rather than quilted, use a heavier thread, such as coton perlé, coton à broder or stranded embroidery cotton.

EQUIPMENT

There are some essential pieces of equipment that have revolutionized the making of patchwork. Rotary cutting equipment, consisting of a rotary cutter used with an acrylic ruler and self-healing cutting mat, has speeded up the process of cutting shapes and made it more accurate; the sewing machine makes assembling the patchwork and quilting the finished piece quick and easy.

SEWING MACHINES

The first sewing machine for the home was patented in 1851, and the electric version was made in 1889, although it wasn't in general use until the 1920s when electricity in the home was more widespread. Ever more sophisticated, computerized machines are now available, but even a machine with just a straight stitch will speed up the process of assembling and quilting the patchwork considerably. Most sewing machines have a swing needle which allows the zigzag stitching used for securing appliqué patches. Machines with decorative stitches give the opportunity to make interesting quilting patterns, as in the wave pattern used for the "Candy Bars" quilt (see pages 32–37).

LONGARM QUILTING MACHINES

These are relatively new machines used by professional quilters. You can choose from a huge library of quilting designs. There is also the option to have edge-to-edge quilting: all-over quilting of one design over the entire quilt, or a combination of patterns to complement each other, e.g. medallions, feathers, cables and cross-hatching. Alternatively, you can specify your own freehand style.

One of the advantages of this machine is that the quilt sandwich does not need to be tacked or pinned together prior to quilting: the pieced top, batting and backing are mounted onto separate rollers which are part of the frame of the machine.

The machine is hand operated and takes considerable skill to operate successfully. Most of the quilters who offer these services advertize in patchwork magazines.

ROTARY CUTTING

Rotary cutting has become the most commonly used method of cutting fabrics for patchwork.

Rotary Cutters

There are several different makes available, mainly in three different sizes: small, medium and large. The medium size ($1\frac{3}{4}$ inches) is probably the one most widely used and perhaps the easiest to control. The smallest can be difficult to use with rulers. The largest is very useful when cutting through several layers of fabric but can take some practice to use. The rotary blade is extremely sharp, so be sure to observe the safety instructions given on the opposite page. But it does become blunted with frequent use, which makes cutting both hazardous and ineffective, so be sure to have replacement blades available for a large patchwork project.

Rulers

Various different rulers are available for use with rotary cutters. These are made of acrylic and are sufficiently thick to act as a guide for the rotary blade. You must use these rulers with the rotary cutter. Do not use metal rulers, as they will severely damage the blades.

The rulers are marked with measurements and angled lines used as a guide when cutting the fabrics. Ideally these markings should be on the underside of the ruler, laser printed and easy to read. Angles should be marked in both directions. Different makes of rulers can have the lines printed in different colors. Choose one that you find easy on your eyes. Some makes also have a non-slip surface on the back – a very helpful addition.

To start, the two most useful basic rulers are either a 24 x 6 in/ 60 x 15 cm or one that is slightly shorter and the small bias square ruler, $6\frac{1}{2}$ in/15 cm. This ruler is particularly useful for marking squares containing two triangles – the half-square triangle units. There are many other rulers designed for specific jobs that you can purchase if and when needed.

Self-Healing Rotary Cutting Mats

These are an essential companion to the rotary cutter and ruler. Do not attempt to cut on any other surface. The mats come in a number of different sizes and several different colors. The smaller ones are useful to take to classes or workshops, but for use at home, purchase the largest that you feel you can afford and that suits your own workstation. It is easier and faster to be able to cut long strips in one go, rather than having to move the fabric up halfway through cutting to fit a smaller board. There is usually a grid on one side of the mat, although both sides can be used. The lines on the mat are not always accurate, so get into the habit of using the lines on the ruler rather than the ones on the mat. Most rotary cutting tools are available with either imperial or metric measurements.

AUXILIARY EQUIPMENT

Most other pieces of equipment are those that you will already have in your workbox. Those listed below are essential, but there is also a vast array of special tools devised by experienced quiltmakers which have specific uses. They are not needed by the beginner quilter but can really enhance the type of designs you can make once you've been bitten by the bug.

Scissors: Two pairs are needed. One large pair of good quality scissors should be used exclusively for cutting fabric. The second smaller pair is for cutting paper, cardboard or template plastic.

Markers: Quilting designs can be traced or drawn on the fabric prior to the layering, or added after the layering, with the aid of stencils or templates. Various marking tools are available: 2H pencils, silver, yellow, white pencils; fade-away or washable marking pens. Whatever your choice, test the markers on a scrap of the fabric used in the quilt to ensure that the marks can be removed.

Pins: Good quality, clean, rustproof, straight pins are essential when a pin is required to hold the work in place for piecing. Flat-headed flower pins are useful because they don't add bulk.

Safety pins: Useful for holding the quilt "sandwich" together for quilting, especially for those who prefer to machine quilt or want the speed of not tacking/basting the three layers together. Place the pins at regular intervals all over the surface.

Needles: For hand quilting use "quilting" or "betweens" needles. Most quilters start with a no. 8 or 9 and progress to a no. 10 or 12. For machine stitching, the needles numbered 70/10 or 80/12 are both suitable for piecing and quilting. Some makers have needles that are labeled "quilting." For tying with thicker thread, use a crewel or embroidery needle.

Thimbles: Two thimbles will be required for hand quilting. One thimble is worn on the hand pushing the needle and the other on the hand underneath the quilt "receiving" the needle. There are various types on the market, ranging from metal to plastic to leather sheaths for the finger. There are also little patches that stick to the finger to protect it. Whichever type you choose it is strongly advised that you do use protection for the fingers on both hands.

HOOPS AND FRAMES

These are needed only if you are quilting by hand. They hold a section of the quilt under light tension to help you to achieve an even stitch. There are many types and sizes available, ranging from round and oval hoops to standing frames made of plastic pipes and wooden fixed frames.

Hoops are perhaps the easiest for a beginner. The 14 in/35 cm or 16 in/40 cm are best for portability. Many quilters continue to use hoops in preference to standing frames. When the quilt is in the hoop the surface of the quilt should not be taut, as is the case with embroidery. If you place the quilt top with its hoop on a table, you should be able to push the fabric in the center of the hoop with your finger and touch the table beneath. Without this "give" you will not be able to "rock" the needle for the quilting stitch. Do not leave the quilt in a hoop when you are not working on it, as the hoop will distort the fabrics.

SAFETY

All rotary cutters have some form of safety mechanism which should always be used. Close the safety cover over the blade after every cut you make, whether or not you intend to continue with another cut. Safety habits are essential and will help prevent accidents. Ensure that the cutters are safely stored out of the reach of children.

Keep the cutter clean and free of fluff. An occasional drop of sewing machine oil helps it to rotate smoothly. Avoid running over pins as this ruins the blade. Renew the blade as soon as it becomes blunt, as a blunt blade makes for inaccurate and difficult cutting and can damage the cutting mat. Replacement blades are readily available, and there are also blade sharpening/exchange services.

TECHNIQUES

ROTARY CUTTING

The basis of rotary cutting is that fabric is cut first in strips – most commonly across the width of the fabric, then cross-cut into patches. Unless otherwise stated, fabric is used folded selvage to selvage, right sides together, as it has come off the bolt. Before any accurate cutting can be done, the first step is to make sure the edge of the fabric is straight.

MAKING THE EDGE STRAIGHT

1 Place the folded fabric on the cutting mat with the selvages at the top and the bulk of the fabric on the side that is not your cutting hand. Place the ruler on the fabric next to the cut edge, aligning the horizontal lines on the ruler with the fold of the fabric and with the selvage.

2 Place your non-cutting hand on the ruler to hold it straight and apply pressure. Keep the hand holding the ruler in line with the hand cutting the fabric. Place the cutter on the mat just below the fabric and up against the ruler. Start cutting by running the cutter upwards and right next to the edge of the ruler (diagram 1).

diagram 1

3 When the cutter becomes level with your extended fingertips, stop cutting, but leave the cutter in position. Carefully move the hand holding the ruler further along the ruler to keep the applied pressure in the area where the cutting is taking place. Continue cutting and moving the steadying hand as necessary until you have cut completely across the fabric. As soon as the cut is complete, close the safety shield on the cutter. If you run out of cutting mat, you will need to reposition the fabric, but this is not ideal as it can bring the fabric out of alignment.

4 Open out the narrow strip of fabric just cut off. Check to make sure that a "valley" or a "hill" has not appeared at the point of the fold on the edge just cut; it should be perfectly straight. If it is not, the fabric was not folded correctly. Fold the fabric again, making sure that this time the selvages are exactly aligned. Make another cut to straighten the edge and check again.

CUTTING STRIPS

The next stage is to cut strips to the specified measurement. To do this, change the position of the fabric to the opposite side of the board, then use the measurements on the ruler to cut the strips.

1 Place the fabric on the cutting mat on the side of your cutting hand. Place the ruler on the mat so that it overlaps the fabric. The cut edge of the fabric should be aligned with the vertical line on the ruler that corresponds to the measurement that you wish to cut. The horizontal lines on the ruler should be aligned with the folded edge and the selvage of the fabric.

2 As before, place one hand on the ruler to apply pressure while cutting the fabric with the other hand (diagram 2).

diagram 2

CROSS-CUTTING

The strips can now be cut into smaller units, whether squares or rectangles. These units are sometimes sub-cut into triangles.

Squares

1 Place the strip just cut on the cutting mat with the longest edge horizontal to you. Cut off the selvages in the same way as you straightened the fabric edge at the start of the process.

2 Now place the strip on the opposite side of the mat and cut across (cross-cut) the strip, using the same measurement on the rule as used for cutting the strip. Be sure that the horizontal lines of the ruler align with the horizontal edge of the fabric. You have now created a number of squares of the required measurement (diagram 3).

diagram 3

Rectangles

1 First cut a strip as long as the required side measurement for the rectangle. Remove the selvages.

2 Turn the strip to the horizontal position as for the squares.

3 Cross-cut this strip using the other side measurement required for the rectangle. Again, ensure that the horizontal lines of the ruler align with the horizontal cut edges of the strip.

Wide strips

Placing two rulers side by side can aid the cutting of extra wide strips. If you don't have two rulers, place the fabric on the cutting mat in the correct position for cutting. Align the cut edge of the fabric with one of the vertical lines running completely across the cutting board and the folded edge with one of the horizontal lines on the mat. If the measurement does not fall on one of the lines on the cutting mat, use the ruler in conjunction with the cutting mat.

Multi-Strip Units

This two-stage method of cutting strips, then cross-cutting into squares or rectangles, can also be used to speed up the cutting of multi-strip units to provide strip blocks, such as used for Rail Fence.

1 Cut the required number and size of strips and stitch together as per the instructions for the block/quilt you are making. Press the seams and check that they are smooth on the right side of the strip unit with no pleats or folds.

2 Place the unit right side up in the horizontal position on the cutting mat. This time when cutting to the required measurement, there are more reference points to ensure that you are cutting straight. Align the horizontal lines on the ruler with the cut edges of the strips and with the seam lines just created (diagram 4). If after cutting a few cross-cuts the lines on the ruler do not line up with the cut edges as well as the seam lines, re-cut the end to straighten it before cutting any more units.

diagram 4

ROTARY CUTTING TRIANGLES

Squares can be divided into either two or four triangles, and it is the combination of fabrics in these squares and the way they are positioned next to each other which provide many fascinating patchwork designs and variations. Both sizes of triangles can be quickly cut using the rotary cutter, or they can be made even faster by a quick piecing method described on page 13.

Cutting Half-Square Triangles

1 Cut the fabric into strips of the correct depth and remove the selvages.

2 Cut the strips into squares of the correct width.

3 Align the 45° angle line on the ruler with the sides of the square, and place the edge of the ruler so that it goes diagonally across the square from corner to corner. Cut the square on this diagonal, creating two half-square triangles (diagram 5).

diagram 5

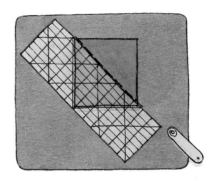

Cutting Quarter-Square Triangles

1 Cut the fabric into strips of the correct depth and remove the selvages.

2 Cut the strips into squares of the correct width.

3 Align the 45° angle line on the ruler with the sides of the square, and place the edge of the ruler so that it goes diagonally across the square from corner to corner. Cut the square on this diagonal, creating two half-square triangles.

4 You can either repeat this procedure on the other diagonal, or, if you are wary of the fabric slipping now that it is in two pieces, separate the two triangles and cut them individually. Align one of the horizontal lines of the ruler with the long edge of the triangle, the 45° line with the short edge of the triangle and the edge of the ruler placed on the point of the triangle opposite the long edge. Cut this half-square triangle into two quarter-square triangles.

diagram 6

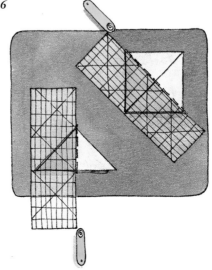

MACHINE STITCHING

> # NOTES
>
> ### Seams
>
> Unless otherwise stated, the seam allowances are included in the measurements given and are always ¼ in for imperial and 0.75 cm for metric. The metric seam allowance is slightly bigger than the imperial, but it is easy to use in conjunction with the various rotary cutting rulers on the market.
>
> ### Measurements
>
> The measurements in the quilt instructions are given in both imperial and metric. Use only one set of measurements in any project – do not interchange them because they are not direct equivalents.

To stitch accurately you must be able to use the correct seam allowance without having to mark it on the fabric. To do this, you use the foot or the bed of your sewing machine as a guide. Many machines today have a "¼ in" or "patchwork" foot available as an extra. There are also various generic foot accessories available which will fit most machines. Before you start any piecing, check that you can make this seam allowance accurately.

Checking the machine for the correct seam allowance

Unthread the machine. Place a piece of paper under the presser foot, so that the righthand edge of the paper aligns with the right-hand edge of the presser foot. Stitch a seam line on the paper. A row of holes will appear. Remove the paper from the machine and measure the distance from the holes to the edge of the paper. If it is not the correct width, try one of the following:

1 If your machine has a number of different needle positions, try moving the needle in the direction required to make the seam allowance accurate. Try the test of stitching a row of holes again.

2 Draw a line on the paper to the correct seam allowance, i.e. ¼ in/0.75 cm from the edge of the paper. Place the paper under the presser foot, aligning the drawn line with the needle. Lower the presser foot to hold the paper securely and, to double-check, lower the needle to ensure that it is directly on top of the drawn line.

Fix a piece of masking tape on the bed of the machine so that the lefthand edge of the tape lines up with the righthand edge of the paper. This can also be done with magnetic strips available on the market to be used as seam guides. But do take advice on using these if your machine is computerized or electronic.

Stitching ¼ in/0.75 cm seams

When stitching pieces together, line the edge of the fabric up with the righthand edge of the presser foot or with the lefthand edge of the tape or the magnetic strip on the bed of your machine, if you have used this method.

Checking the fabric for the correct seam allowance

As so much of the success of a patchwork depends on accuracy of cutting and seaming, it is worth double-checking the fabric to see that you are stitching a ¼ in/0.75 cm seam.

Cut three strips of fabric 1½ in/4 cm wide. Stitch these together. Press the seams away from the center strip. Measure the center strip. It should measure exactly 1 in/2.5 cm wide. If not, reposition the needle/tape and try again.

Stitch length

The stitch length used is normally 12 stitches to the inch or 5 stitches to the centimeter. If the pieces being stitched together are to be cross-cut into smaller units, it is advisable to shorten the stitch slightly, which will mean the seam is less likely to unravel. It is also good practice to start each new project with a new needle in a clean machine – free of fluff around the bobbin housing.

QUICK MACHINE PIECING

Experienced quilters have devised all sorts of ingenious ways of stitching pieces together to speed up the process of making the components of the blocks. The three most basic techniques used here are for stitching pairs of patches together, for stitching half-square triangle units and for stitching quarter-square triangle units.

Chain piecing

Have all the pairs of patches or strips together ready in a pile. Place the first two patches or strips in the machine, right sides together, and stitch them together. Just before reaching the end, stop stitching and pick up the next two patches or strips. Place them on the bed of the machine so that they just touch the patches under the needle. Stitch off one set and onto the next. Repeat this process until all the pairs are stitched to create a "chain" of pieced patches/strips (diagram 7). Cut the thread between each unit to

diagram 7

separate them. Open out and press the seams according to the instructions given with each project.

Stitching Half-square Triangle Units

This is a quick method of creating a bi-colored square without cutting the triangles first.

1 Cut two squares of different colored fabrics to the correct measurement, i.e. the finished size of the bi-colored square plus $\frac{7}{8}$ in/2.5 cm. Place them right sides together aligning all raw edges. On the wrong side of the top square draw a diagonal line from one corner to the other.

2 Stitch $\frac{1}{4}$ in/0.75 cm away from either side of the drawn line.

3 Cut the two halves apart by cutting on the drawn line. Open out and press the seams according to the instructions given with each project (diagram 8). You now have two squares each containing two triangles.

Stitching Quarter-Square Triangle Units

This method also creates triangles from squares without first cutting the triangles.

1 Cut squares to the finished size of a square containing four triangles plus $1\frac{1}{4}$ in/3.5 cm. Follow the stitching, cutting-apart and pressing sequence as for the half-square triangle units.

2 Place the two bi-coloured squares right sides together. Ensure that each triangle is not facing a triangle of the same color. Draw a line diagonally from corner to corner, at right angles to the stitched seam.

3 Pin carefully to match the seams, then stitch $\frac{1}{4}$ in/0.75 cm away from either side of this drawn line. Before cutting apart, open up each side and check to see that the points match in the center. Cut apart on the drawn line. You now have two squares each containing four triangles (diagram 9).

diagram 8

diagram 9

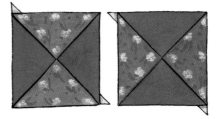

PRESSING

Each individual project will have instructions about the direction in which to press the seam allowances. These have been designed to facilitate easier piecing at junctions and to reduce the bulk so that seam allowances do not lay one on top of the other. Pressing as you complete each stage of the piecing will also improve the accuracy and look of your work. Take care not to distort the patches. Be gentle, not fierce, with the iron.

ASSEMBLING THE QUILT

Most patchwork tops are framed by one or more borders. The simplest method of adding borders is to add strips first to the top and bottom of the quilt and then to the sides, producing abutted corners. A more complicated method is to add strips to adjacent sides and to join them with seams at 45 degrees, giving mitered borders. Only the first method is used for the quilts in this book.

ADDING BORDERS WITH ABUTTED CORNERS

The measurements for the borders required for each quilt in the book will be given in the instructions. It is, however, always wise to measure your own work to determine the actual measurement.

1 Measure the quilt through the center across the width, edge to edge. Cut the strips for the top and bottom borders to this length by the width required for the border.

2 Pin the strips to the quilt by pinning first at each end, then in the middle, then evenly spaced along the edge. By pinning in this manner it is possible to ensure that the quilt "fits" the border. Stitch the border strips into position on the top and bottom edge of the quilt (diagram 10). Press the seams towards the border.

diagram 10

3 Measure the quilt through the center top to bottom. Cut the side border strips to this measurement.

4 Pin and stitch the borders to each side of the quilt as before (diagram 11). Press the seams towards the border.

diagram 11

QUILTING

The three layers or "sandwich" of the backing/batting/pieced top are held together by quilting or by tying. The quilting can be done either by hand or machine. The tying is done by hand by stitching decorative ties at strategic points on the quilt. Buttons can also be used for the same purpose.

Layering/Sandwiching

Prior to any quilting, unless you are using a longarm quilting machine (see page 8), the pieced top must be layered with the batting and the backing. The batting and the backing should be slightly larger than the quilt top – approximately 2 in/5 cm on all sides. If the quilt edges are to be finished with a binding, the three layers are assembled in the order that they will appear in the finished quilt, i.e. backing at the bottom, batting in the middle and patchwork on top. If there is no binding, the sequence before stitching together is: backing fabric, patchwork, then batting.

Assembling prior to binding

1 Lay out the backing fabric wrong side up. Ensure that it is stretched out and smooth. Secure the edges with masking tape placed at intervals along the edges to help to hold it in position.
2 Place the batting on top of the backing fabric. If you need to join two pieces of batting first, do so by abutting the edges and stitching together by hand using a herringbone stitch (diagram 12).

diagram 12

3 Place the pieced top right side up and centered on top of the batting.

Assembling where no binding is used

1 Spread out the batting on a flat surface. Smooth out to ensure there are no wrinkles.
2 Place the backing fabric centrally on top of the batting, right side up.
3 Place the pieced top centrally over the backing, wrong side up. Pin with straight pins around the edges to keep them together.
4 Stitch around all four sides with a $\frac{1}{4}$ in/0.75 cm seam allowance, but leaving an opening of about 15–18 in/35–45 cm along one of the sides.

5 Trim away excess batting across the corners to reduce bulk, then turn the quilt right side out so that the batting is now in the middle. Slip-stitch the opening closed.
6 Smooth out the layers of the quilt, then roll and finger-press the edges so that the seam lies along the edge or just underneath.

Basting prior to quilting

If the piece is to be quilted rather than tied, the three layers now need to be held together at regular intervals. This can be done by basting or by using safety pins. For either method, start in the center of the quilt and work out to the edges.

Using a long length of thread start basting in the center of the quilt top. Pull only about half of the thread through as you start stitching. Once you have reached the edge, go back and thread the other end of the thread and baste to the opposite edge. Repeat this process, stitching in a grid over the whole quilt top (diagram 13).

diagram 13

MACHINE QUILTING

Designs to be used for machine quilting should ideally be those that have one continuous line. The lines can be straight or free form curves and squiggles. For either type, be sure to keep the density of stitching the same. With either method, continuous lines of stitching will be visible both on the top and on the back of the quilt. It is a quick method but requires careful preparation.

There is a wide variety of tools available designed to help make handling the quilt easier during the machine quilting process. But the most essential requirement is practice.

It is worth making up a practice sandwich – if possible using the same fabrics and batting as used in the actual quilt – to be sure that you get the effect you want. In any case, plan the quilting design first; otherwise there is a danger that you will start with quite dense stitching, then tire of the process and begin to space out the lines, producing an uneven pattern.

When starting and stopping the stitching during machine quilting, either reduce the stitch length to zero or stitch several stitches in one spot. If you do not like the buildup of stitches that this method produces, leave long tails on the thread when you start and stop. Later, pull these threads through to one side of the quilt, knot them, then thread them into a needle. Push the needle into the fabric and into the batting, but not through to the other side of the quilt, and then back out through the fabric again, about 1 in/2.5 cm away from where the needle entered the quilt. Cut off the excess thread.

Straight Line Machine Quilting

One of the easiest and most common forms of straight line quilting is called "in-the-ditch." It involves stitching just beside a seam line on the side without the seam allowances. Some machines require a walking foot to stitch the three layers together. These are used with the feed dogs up, and, while in use, the machine controls the direction and stitch length.

Free Motion Machine Quilting

When machine quilting in freehand, a darning foot is used with the feed dogs down, so that you can move the quilt forwards, backwards and sideways. This is easier on some machines than others, but all require a bit of practice.

Hand Quilting

The stitch used for hand quilting is a running stitch. The needle goes into the quilt through to the back and returns to the top of the quilt all in one movement. The aim is to have the size of the stitches and spaces between them the same.

1 Thread a needle with an 18 in/45 cm length of quilting thread and knot the end. Push the needle into the fabric and into the batting, but not through to the back, about 1 in/2.5 cm away from where you want to start stitching. Bring the needle up through the fabric at the point where you will begin stitching. Gently pull on the thread to "pop" the knot through into the batting.

2 To make a perfect quilting stitch the needle needs to enter the fabric perpendicular to the quilt top. Holding the needle between your first finger and thumb, push the needle into the fabric until it hits the thimble on the finger of the hand underneath.

3 The needle can now be held between the thimble on your sewing hand and the thimble on the finger underneath. Release your thumb and first finger hold on the needle. Place your thumb on the quilt top just in front of the position where the needle will come back up to the top and gently press down on the quilt top (diagram 14).

diagram 14

4 At the same time, rock the thread end of the needle back down towards the quilt top and push the needle up from underneath so that the point appears on the top of the quilt. You can either pull the needle through, now making only one stitch, or rock the needle up to the vertical again, push the needle into the quilt top, then rock the needle back down to the quilt top again, placing another stitch on the needle. Repeat until you can no longer rock the needle into a completely upright position (diagram 15). Pull the needle through the quilt. One stitch at a time, or several placed on

diagram 15

the needle at once – "the rocking stitch" – before pulling the thread through, are both acceptable.

5 When the stitching is complete, tie a knot in the thread close to the quilt surface. Push the needle into the quilt top and the batting, next to the knot but not through to the back of the quilt. Bring the needle up again about 1 in/2.5 cm away and gently tug on the thread to "pop" the knot through the fabric and into the batting. Cut the thread.

Big Stitch Quilting

For these super quick quilts, another form of hand quilting, known as "Big Stitch," is used, which speeds up the process of quilting by hand and adds another design element. Big Stitch uses coton perlé no. 8 thread and a larger needle with a bigger eye. The stitches are also larger, and the quilting designs simpler. The quilting stitch for the "Big Stitch" is also a running stitch.

BINDING

Once the quilting is completed, the quilt is usually (but not always) finished off with a binding to enclose the raw edges. This binding can be cut on the straight or on the bias. Either way, the binding is usually best done with a double fold. It can be applied in four separate pieces to each of the four sides, or the binding strips can be joined together and stitched to the quilt in one continuous strip with mitered corners. To join straight-cut pieces for a continuous strip, use straight seams; to join bias-cut pieces, use diagonal seams (diagram 16).

diagram 16

For either method, the width of the bias strips should be cut to the following measurement: finished binding width x four + the seam allowance x two.
For example:
A finished binding width of $\frac{1}{2}$ in would be cut as $2\frac{1}{2}$ in:
$(\frac{1}{2}$ in x 4) + $(\frac{1}{4}$ in x 2) = $2\frac{1}{2}$ in
or 1.25 cm would be cut 6.5 cm:
(1.25 cm x 4) + (0.75 cm x 2) = 6.5 cm

Binding the four sides separately

1 Cut binding strips to the required width. Fold in half lengthwise with wrong sides together and lightly press.

2 Measure the quilt through the center from top to bottom and cut two of the binding strips to this length.

3 Pin one of the strips down the side of the quilt, right sides together, and align raw edges. Stitch with the usual seam allowance.

4 Fold the binding strip to the back of the quilt, turn under a $\frac{1}{4}$ in/ 0.75 cm hem and slip-stitch to the backing fabric. Trim the ends level with the batting. Do the same on the opposite side of the quilt with the other strip.

5 Measure the quilt through the center from side to side and add $1\frac{1}{2}$ in/4 cm for turnings. Cut two more binding strips to this length, joining if necessary. Stitch to the top and bottom of the quilt, turning in a short hem at either end before folding to the back and slip-stitching down. Slip-stitch the corners neatly.

Continuous strip binding

1 Fold the binding in half lengthwise with wrong sides together and lightly press.

2 Place the binding's raw edges along the raw edge of the quilt – somewhere along one side, not at a corner. Begin stitching about 1 in/2.5 cm from the end of the binding, and, using $\frac{1}{4}$ in/0.75 cm seam allowance, stitch the binding to the quilt through all layers of the "sandwich" stopping $\frac{1}{4}$ in/0.75 cm from the end. At this point, backstitch to secure, then break off the threads. Remove the quilt from the sewing machine.

3 Place the quilt on a flat surface with the binding stitched just at the top edge, then fold the binding strip up and away from the quilt to "twelve o'clock," creating a 45° fold at the corner (diagram 17).

diagram 17

4 Fold the binding back down to "six o'clock," aligning the raw edges of the binding to the raw edge of the quilt. The fold created on the binding at the top should be the same distance away from the seam as the width of the finished binding. i.e. ½ in/1.25 cm from seam line to fold (diagram 18).

diagram 18

5 Start stitching the binding to the quilt at the same point the previous stitching stopped, ¼ in/0.75 cm from the edge of the quilt top. Secure with backstitching, then continue to the next corner. Repeat the process at each corner.

6 Stop about 2 in/5 cm from where you started. Open the fold out on both ends of the binding, then seam the two ends together. Trim away the excess, refold and finish applying the binding to the quilt.

7 Trim the excess batting and backing fabric so that the distance from the stitching line equals, or is slightly wider than, that of the finished binding. Fold the binding over to the back and hand stitch the folded edge of the binding to the quilt along the row of machine stitching just created. A miter will appear at the corners on the front and on the back of the binding. Slip-stitch these in place (diagram 19).

diagram 19

HANGING SLEEVE

If your quilt is a wallhanging or is to be exhibited it will need a hanging sleeve. A sleeve can be added after the quilt is completely finished, but a more secure and permanent sleeve can be added along with the binding. Stitch the binding to the front of the quilt and, before folding it over onto the back, add the sleeve.

1 Cut a piece of fabric, preferably matching the backing, to measure 10 in/25 cm high, and as long as the quilt is wide. Make a 1 in/2.5 cm hem on both the short ends.

2 Fold the fabric in half along the length with wrong sides together. Center this on the back of the quilt, aligning the raw edges of the sleeve with the raw edges of the quilt. Secure with pins (diagram 20).

diagram 20

3 Turn the quilt over so the front is face up. Taking care to remove the pins as you approach them, stitch the sleeve to the quilt by stitching along the row of stitching made when applying the binding.

4 Finish hand stitching on the binding.

5 Lay the quilt on a flat surface with the back face up. Gently roll the top layer of the tube up to the top edge of the binding so it forms a fold along this edge. Secure with pins. Now smooth out the rest of the sleeve tube until it rests evenly on the back of the quilt (diagram 21).

diagram 21

6 Stitch the sleeve to the back of the quilt along the fold at the bottom of the sleeve, and at each end, so that when a rod is inserted it will not actually touch the back of the quilt but only the sleeve fabric. Take care that your stitches only go into the back and batting of the quilt and are not visible on the front. Remove the pins. The sleeve is now stitched to the quilt and has a slight bulge in it. This bulge will allow room for a rod to go through the sleeve without distorting the quilt when it is hung.

LABELING

Your quilt should be signed and dated and should include the place where it was made. This provides a record for your own information, as well as for others in the future.

The details can be incorporated on the quilt front or on a label attached to the back. This label can be simply handwritten with a permanent pen or made very elaborate with pieced, embroidered or fabric painting. Another way of making an individual label is with the help of a computer and color printer.

TIPS

Strip cutting

To cut strips longer than the length of a ruler, fold the strip in half and cut half the length. To cut strips wider than the width of a ruler, either use two rulers side by side, or use the markings on the cutting mat plus the ruler, although this is not quite as accurate.

Chain-piecing

To further speed up this process, place the two pieces/strips to be stitched together beside the sewing machine. Place one group of patches facing up and one group facing down. Now when you pick up one piece, its partner is in the correct position to place on top with right sides together.

Pressing seams

Always press seams to one side unless otherwise stated, because an open seam is put under more strain. Press fabrics towards the darker fabric to prevent show-through.

Slip-stitched seams

For quilts that are made without a binding, you can finish the slip-stitched seam neatly before you turn your quilt by stitching across the turning opening using the longest stitch your machine will make. Finger-press the seam allowance open quite firmly. Now rip out the long stitches, turn the quilt and you will find you have an obvious straight crease line to follow when hand stitching.

Measuring borders

Even if measurements are given for border strips, it is always worth double-checking against your own pieced top. Measure through the middle of the quilt since the edges can become stretched.

Attaching borders

Once you have determined the size of the top, bottom and side borders, fit the pieced top to these measurements rather than the other way around. Mark the center and quarter points of the borders and of the quilt sides and match them up. You may need to ease the sides of the quilt to fit the borders, but this will help to give a flat square quilt rather than one with wavy borders.

Storage

Store quilts in an old pillowcase or acid-free tissue paper rather than in a plastic bag, which doesn't allow fabrics to breathe and therefore encourages mold.

Batik Beauty

Designed by Sarah Wellfair

The batik fabrics used in this quilt are such beautiful patterns, that cutting them into smaller pieces would have lost the impact of the designs. I chose to alternate the plain batiks with the simple four-patch block to provide a contrast and to single out some of the vibrant colors.

Finished size: 42½ x 36½ in/108 x 93 cm

MATERIALS
Blocks: 6 fat or long quarters of different batik designs and colors. I used four green/turquoise designs plus an orange and a pink for accent colors.
Border: dark blue or other contrasting color, 20 in/50 cm

Batting: lightweight cotton, 1¼ yds x 45 in/ 1 m x 115 cm wide
Backing: coordinating batik, 1¼ yds x 45 in/ 1 m x 115 cm wide
Machine quilting thread: purple metallic
Binding: 20 in/50 cm

ALTERNATIVE COLOR SCHEMES

1 For a child's room, a bright selection of children's prints and coordinating plaids; 2 This block uses the same fabric pattern but in three different color-ways to give a bright, unified design; 3 The large squares are cut from a pretty butterfly print with four contrasting fabrics for the four-patch to give a really sunny design; 4 A selection of hand-dyed fabrics gives a soft and completely different look.

1

2

3

4

CUTTING

1 From each of the fat quarters, cut ten $3\frac{1}{2}$ in/9 cm squares, then cut a total of fifteen $6\frac{1}{2}$ in/16.5 cm squares from the remaining pieces.

2 From the border fabric, cut four strips $3\frac{1}{2}$ in/9 cm deep across the width of the fabric.

3 From the binding fabric, cut four strips 3 in/7.5 cm deep across the width of the fabric.

STITCHING

1 Sort the $3\frac{1}{2}$ in/9 cm squares into pairs of colors – you can vary the combinations but you need two pairs the same for each four-patch block. Place one of each color right sides together and pin and stitch making a $\frac{1}{4}$ in/0.75 cm seam allowance. Repeat with the remaining squares. Press the seams toward the darker fabric. You should have 30 pairs (diagram 1).

diagram 1

2 Take two matching pairs, place right sides together, reversing the colors, and pin carefully, matching center seams. Stitch together with the usual seam allowance (diagram 2). Repeat to make 15 four-patch blocks.

3 Following the quilt assembly plan on page 22, lay out the four-patch blocks alternating with the plain blocks until you are satisfied with the arrangement – you should have five blocks across and six down.

diagram 2

NOTE If you press the seam allowances in opposite directions, the center should lock together.

4 Working on the two vertical rows on the lefthand side of the arrangement, chain-piece the blocks together in pairs (diagram 3). Cut, open out and press the seams towards the solid blocks, then replace in the correct positions in the quilt plan.

diagram 3

5 Repeat with vertical rows three and four.

6 Pin and stitch the units together in horizontal rows, adding the single block from column five at the end of each row (diagram 4). Then pin and stitch the horizontal rows together, being careful to match the seams. Press the seams towards the top row. The quilt should now measure approximately $30\frac{1}{2}$ x $36\frac{1}{2}$ in/ 76.5 x 91.5 cm.

diagram 4

7 Measure the pieced top through the center from side to side for an accurate measurement, then trim two of the border strips to this measurement. Stitch to the top and bottom of the quilt. Press towards the border.

8 Measure the pieced top through the center from top to bottom, then trim the remaining two border strips to this measurement. Stitch to the sides and press towards the border.

FINISHING

1 Measure the patchwork top and give it a final pressing.

2 Cut the batting and backing 2 in/5 cm bigger all around than the finished patchwork size.

3 Spread the backing right side down on a flat surface, then smooth the batting and the patchwork top, right side up, on top. Fasten together with safety pins or baste in a grid.

4 Machine quilt as desired. I have used a free motion quilting design with a heart motif, and stitched with a purple metallic thread.

6 Trim the excess batting and backing level with the patchwork top.

7 Cut the binding fabric into strips 3 in/7.5 cm deep across the width of fabric. Fold in half lengthwise, wrong sides together and press.

8 Measure the quilt through the center from top to bottom, and cut two of the binding strips to this length. Pin one strip to the side of the quilt, matching raw edges. Stitch approximately ½ in/1.5 cm in from the edge. Fold over to the back of the quilt and slip-stitch down. Do the same on the opposite side of the quilt with the remaining strip.

9 Measure the quilt through the center from side to side, and add 1½ in/4 cm to this for turning. Cut two more binding strips to this length. Stitch to the top and bottom of the quilt, turning in a short hem at either end before folding to the back.

Blooming Borders

Designed by Sharon Chambers

It's summertime and the herbaceous borders are bursting with beautiful blooms. Take time to enjoy them with lunch on the lawn seated around this charming quilt. The design is so quick and easy you'll be delighted with how fast it grows! Make one as a gift in the lucky recipient's favorite flower shades and present it tucked inside a picnic basket.

Finished size: 54 x 42 in/135 x 105 cm

All fabrics used in the quilt top are 45 in/115 cm wide, 100% cotton.

Main fabric A for center rectangle and outer borders: 55 in/1.4 m

Fabric B for first and third narrow borders: 24 in/60 cm

Fabric C for second narrow border: 15 in/40 cm

Fabric marker

Binding: striped fabric, 20 in/50 cm

Backing: 45 x 56 in/115 x 150 cm

Batting: 100% cotton, 45 x 56 in/115 x 150 cm

Cotton quilting thread: to match or tone with top

ALTERNATIVE COLOR SCHEMES

Roses were the inspiration behind the original quilt but you could just as well choose different flowers for your color scheme. 1 These bright blues and yellows come from a border of forget-me-nots and tulips; 2 The small flower print is matched with a soft check and calico reminiscent of a cottage garden; 3 The reds, rusts and golds are a reminder of the stunning shades of autumn; 4 This final color scheme is chosen to match a blue and white set of china.

1

2

3

4

CUTTING

1 From the main fabric **A**, cut four strips across the width of the fabric, 6½ in/16.5 cm deep. Cut these strips down to 42½ in/106.5 cm long. Set aside.

NOTE To cut longer than the length of your ruler, fold the strip in half and cut half the finished length.

2 From the remainder of fabric **A**, cut a center rectangle, 18½ x 30½ in/46.5 x 76.5 cm.

3 From fabric **B**, cut eight strips across the width of the fabric, 2½ in/6.5 cm deep. Trim two of these strips to 22½ in/56.5 cm long, four strips to 30½ in/76.5 cm long, and the remaining two strips to 38½ in/96.5 cm long. Set aside.

4 From fabric **C**, cut four strips across the width of the fabric, 2½ in/6.5 cm deep. Trim two of these strips to 26½ in/66.5 cm long and two to 34½ in/86.5 cm long. Set aside.

5 For the binding, lay the striped fabric out flat. Starting in the lower lefthand corner make the first diagonal cut on the true 45 degree bias of the fabric. Discard the corner triangle. Measuring from the diagonal edge of the fabric, cut eight strips 1½ in/4 cm wide (diagram 1). Be careful not to stretch these strips. Set aside.

diagram 1

STITCHING

1 Using the usual ¼ in/0.75 cm seam, pin and stitch one of the 30½ in/76.5 cm border strips cut from fabric **B** to one of the long sides of the center rectangle (diagram 2a). Repeat for the opposite side (diagram 2b). Press the seams towards the border strips. Pin and stitch one of the 22½ in/56.5 cm strips of fabric **B** to the top of the center rectangle (diagram 2c) and repeat for the bottom of the rectangle (diagram 2d). Press the seams as before.

diagram 2a

diagram 2b

diagram 2c

diagram 2d

2 Pin and stitch the two 34½ in/86.5 cm long strips cut from fabric **C** to the sides of the rectangular panel, pressing the seams as before. Stitch the 26½ in/66.5 cm strips of fabric **C** to the top and bottom. Press the seams.

3 From the remaining narrow border strips cut from fabric **B**, stitch the 38½ in/96.5 cm long strips to the sides first, then the 30½ in/76.5 cm strips to the top and bottom, pressing as usual.

4 Lastly, stitch the 6½ in/16.5 cm deep borders of fabric **A** to the sides, top and bottom, pressing as usual.

NOTE To make sure you don't stretch the borders out of shape while stitching them, mark and pin the center, the quarter points and both ends.

FINISHING

1 Mark the quilting lines as shown in diagram 3 on the finished top, using an appropriate marker for the color of your fabrics. The simple straight quilting lines made up of concentric 2 in/5 cm wide rectangles echo the size and shape of the narrow borders.

diagram 3

2 Measure the patchwork top and cut the batting and backing fabric at least 1 in/2.5 cm larger all around.

3 Spread the backing right side down on a flat surface, then smooth the batting and the patchwork top, right side up, on top. Fasten together with safety pins.

4 Using a walking foot, machine quilt through all three layers. With the walking foot still attached, stitch a line of stay-stitching around the outside of the quilt ¼ in/0.75 cm in from the edge to stabilize it.

5 Join the binding strips with diagonal seams to make a continuous length to fit all around the quilt. Use it to bind the edges with a single-fold binding, mitered at the corners.

Candy Bars

Designed by Jean Hunt

Hot pink fabric frames the colorful bars in this topper for a single bed. Very simple blocks are joined together in rows to make the bars, reminiscent of the most colorful jars in a candy shop. Simple quilting completes the project, which takes just 12 hours to make.

Finished size: 59 x 47 in/150 x 120 cm

MATERIALS
All fabrics used in the quilt top are 45 in/115 cm wide, 100% cotton.

For the center bars: 6½ in/17 cm of at least nine different small-patterned or cloudy fabrics in pinks, oranges and mauves. These should be of approximately the same value, i.e. light or medium, and preferably not too dark.

For the border and the plain bars: hot pink, 60 in/153 cm. This should be darker than the fabric for the "candy" colored bars.
Binding: pink pattern, 7½ in/20 cm
Backing: 100% cotton or sheeting, 63 x 51 in/ 160 x 130 cm
Batting: 2 oz polyester batting or a cotton alternative, 63 x 51 in/160 x 130 cm
Machine quilting thread: to match, preferably cotton

ALTERNATIVE COLOR SCHEMES

1 Dark center strips with a light border reverse the color scheme, making the bars more prominent; 2 The cream and gold combination is a sophisticated colorway; 3 Blues and greens make a cool alternative; 4 Different shades of denim make a good color scheme for a teenager.

1

2

3

4

CUTTING

1 From the nine strips for the center bars, remove the selvage, then cut 49 rectangles measuring 7 x 6½ in/18 x 16.5 cm.

2 From the hot pink fabric, cut four strips, 3½ in/9 cm deep and approximately 60 in/153 cm wide, and six strips, 2½ in/6.5 cm deep and approximately 43 in/109 cm wide.

NOTE You may wish to cut the hot pink strips after construction of the bars, as measurements may vary slightly.

3 Cut the binding fabric into strips, 1½ in/4 cm deep across the width.

STITCHING

1 Take your pile of 49 rectangles to the cutting board. Choose two different colors. Take the first rectangle and place it on the cutting board right side up, with the longer edge at the top. Take the second rectangle and place it on top of the first rectangle, also right side up. Using a rotary ruler and cutter, cut at an angle (approximately 60 degrees) from part way along the bottom long edge to the top long edge of the rectangles (you can use the markings on your ruler if you have them), thus splitting the rectangles into two pieces (diagram 1).

diagram 1

2 Take the lefthand piece of the first fabric rectangle and place it next to the righthand piece of the second fabric rectangle to form the first block. Stitch together by placing the two halves right sides together, aligning the raw edges and stitching a ¼ in/0.75 cm seam. Line up the tops of the two halves as accurately as possible. Repeat with the remaining two pieces to make your second block. The block should measure 6½ x 6½ in/16.5 x 16.5 cm.

3 Continue as above until all 49 blocks have been completed. Varying the angle of cut slightly each time gives a more interesting look, but be careful not to mix up the pieces when cut – pin together if not stitching right away. When complete, press lightly.

4 Sort the blocks out on the floor, in seven rows each with seven blocks, until you are happy with the placement. Number the blocks, so that they do not become muddled.

5 Following the quilt assembly diagram on page 34, rotate each block 90 degrees to its neighbor, then pin and stitch together in rows, using the usual seam allowance, and press.

6 To add the sashing strips, place a strip of 2½ in/6.5 cm deep hot pink fabric along the top of the bottom strip of blocks, right sides together, the raw edges aligned. Pin carefully (the patchwork strips will stretch more than the plain strips), then stitch (diagram 2). Press the seams towards the sashing.

diagram 2

7 Place the next strip of blocks along the top of the pink sashing strip, right sides together, with the raw edges aligned. Pin and stitch. Press.

8 Repeat steps 6 and 7 until the seven strips of blocks have been joined with sashing strips in between.

ADDING THE BORDERS

1 Measure the pieced top through the center from side to side, then trim two of the 3½ in/9 cm deep hot pink strips to this measurement. Pin and stitch to the top and bottom of the quilt.

2 Measure the pieced top through the center from top to bottom, then trim the remaining two hot pink strips to this measurement. Pin and stitch to the sides.

FINISHING

1 Spread the backing right side down on a flat surface, then smooth the batting and the patchwork top, right side up, on top. Fasten together with safety pins or baste in a grid.

2 Using a walking foot and the decorative stitches on your sewing machine, ideally a scallop or wave pattern, machine quilt in lines down and across the quilt, as desired.

3 Trim off any excess batting and backing, so that they are even with the pieced top. Join the binding strips with diagonal seams to make a continuous length to fit all around the quilt. Use to bind the edges with a double-fold binding, mitered at the corners.

Checks and Flowers

Designed by Rita Whitehorn

This simple design is made from a combination of strips and rectangles, which are quickly stitched together to make a cheerful bed quilt. The white broderie anglaise echoes the floral design in the small prints, and the color scheme is brought together by the strips of plain fabrics in between. The broderie anglaise will need to be backed with a fine lawn or something similar to stop the batting from coming through the holes.

Finished size: 78 x 60 in/198 x 153 cm

MATERIALS
All fabrics used in the patchwork top are
45 in/115 cm wide, 100% cotton.

For the large and small blocks: one fat quarter of six
different colors (**A**, **C**, **D**, **E**, **F** and **G**) (I used three
mainly blue and three mainly yellow), plus ½ yd/50 cm
of broderie anglaise (**B**)

For outer border and infill strips: yellow (**H**),
3 yds/2.75 m
For inner border and infill strips: dark blue (**I**),
¾ yd/70 cm. (An extra ½ yd/50 cm will be needed if
this is used as an unbroken color for binding.)
For infill strips: white (**J**), ¼ yd/25 cm
Backing: coordinating color, 4 yds/3.75 m
Batting: 80% wool and 20% mixed fibers, one piece,
64 x 82 in/163 x 208 cm
For broderie anglaise backing: lawn or a lighter
fabric, ½ yd/50 cm

ALTERNATIVE COLOR SCHEMES

1 Floral fabrics coordinated with a stripe and a solid fabric in pastels make a restful color scheme; 2 To match a natural colored decor, choose green, tan and mustard fabrics; 3 For a boy's bedroom, pick a sporty print and team with bold primaries; 4 The boldness of the striking black floral print is toned down by the more subtle colors in the strips without losing the overall impact of this color scheme.

1

2

3

4

NOTES

Before cutting fabrics it is best to make a plan for the quilt blocks.

Press all seams to the darkest fabric at all times; otherwise they will show through a light fabric. Do not press seams open at any time. This weakens the seams.

If you wish to use a directional print for the large and small blocks, you'll need extra fabric.

CUTTING

1 From the seven fabrics for the large and small blocks, cut the following:

from **A**, three large rectangles, $11\frac{1}{2}$ x $8\frac{1}{2}$ in/ 29 x 21.5 cm, and two small rectangles, $4\frac{1}{2}$ x $8\frac{1}{2}$ in/ 11.5 x 21.5 cm;

from **B**, three large rectangles, $11\frac{1}{2}$ x $8\frac{1}{2}$ in/ 29 x 21.5 cm, and two small rectangles, $4\frac{1}{2}$ x $8\frac{1}{2}$ in/ 11.5 x 21.5 cm;

from **C**, three large rectangles, $11\frac{1}{2}$ x $8\frac{1}{2}$ in/ 29 x 21.5 cm;

from **D**, three large rectangles, $11\frac{1}{2}$ x $8\frac{1}{2}$ in/ 29 x 21.5 cm;

from **E**, two large rectangles, $11\frac{1}{2}$ x $8\frac{1}{2}$ in/ 29 x 21.5 cm;

from **F**, two large rectangles, $11\frac{1}{2}$ x $8\frac{1}{2}$ in/ 29 x 21.5 cm;

from **G**, two large rectangles, $11\frac{1}{2}$ x $8\frac{1}{2}$ in/ 29 x 21.5 cm.

2 From the lawn backing fabric, cut three large rectangles, $11\frac{1}{2}$ x $8\frac{1}{2}$ in/29 x 21.5 cm, and two small rectangles, $4\frac{1}{2}$ x $8\frac{1}{2}$ in/11.5 x 21.5 cm.

3 From each of the yellow, dark blue and white fabrics (**H, I, J**) cut four strips across the width, 2 in/5 cm deep, for the infill strips.

STITCHING

1 Take one each of the yellow, white and dark blue 2 in/5 cm strips and seam together along the long edges. Press the seams away from the white fabric (diagram 1).

diagram 1

2 Repeat with the remaining three strips in each color. Cross-cut these three-color strips into rectangles, $8\frac{1}{2}$ in/21.5 cm wide (diagram 2). This should yield five rectangles from each of the four sets of three strips: 17 rectangles are required for the quilt.

diagram 2

3 Place the lawn backing fabric on the back of each of the broderie anglaise rectangles and tack together.

4 Following the quilt assembly plan on page 40, lay out the large and small rectangles in columns with infill strips in between.

5 Pin and stitch the blocks and infill strips together in columns, then pin and stitch the columns together. Remember to press all seams toward the darker fabrics.

ADDING THE BORDERS

1 For the inner border, measure the pieced top through the center from side to side, then cut two strips to this measurement and 3 in/7.5 cm deep from the remaining dark blue fabric (**I**). Stitch to the top and bottom of the quilt.

2 Measure the pieced top through the center from top to bottom, then cut four strips, 3 in/7.5 cm deep, from the remaining dark blue fabric. Join as necessary to make the required measurement. Pin and stitch to the sides.

3 For the outer border, measure the pieced top through the center from side to side, then cut two strips to this measurement and 8 in/20 cm deep across the width of the remaining yellow fabric (H). Pin and stitch to the top and bottom of the quilt.

4 Measure the pieced top through the center from top to bottom, then cut two strips, 8 in/20 cm deep, down the length of the remaining yellow fabric. Join as necessary to make the required measurement. Pin and stitch to the sides.

FINISHING

1 Measure the completed patchwork top and cut the backing fabric 2 in/5 cm bigger on all four sides. You may need to cut and join the backing fabric to fit.

NOTE Before joining the pieces of backing fabric, cut off the selvage edge, as this does not have any "give" and will create a taut seam. For that reason it is always best to cut off any selvage edge before joining any fabrics.

2 Spread the backing right side down on a flat surface, then smooth the batting and the patchwork top, right side up, on top. Fasten together with safety pins or baste in a grid.

3 Machine or hand quilt two vertical lines down each of the large rectangles and quilt in the ditch along the infill strips.

4 For the binding in a continuous dark blue (I), cut seven strips, 3 in/7.5 cm deep, across the width of the fabric. Cut one strip in half and join each portion to one whole length. Join two of the remaining strips into one whole length and repeat with the final two strips. Use to bind the edges with a double-fold binding, butted up at the corners.

5 Alternatively, to make a random fabric binding as shown in the photograph, you will need to cut strips of fabric from each of the blue fabrics, all 3 in/7.5 cm deep. Join with straight, not diagonal, seams to make four lengths to fit the four sides of the quilt, and use as above.

Crosses and Squares

Designed by Katharine Guerrier

The accent is on economy both in time and expense for this quilt. The squares cut for the blocks are designed to make the best use of the fabric width, and quick piecing techniques ensure that the blocks grow quickly. I pieced the backing from a "collage" of fabric pieces and blocks left over from other projects, but I've given the measurements for using a single piece of fabric in the instructions. The quilting was done on a longarm quilting machine by Jan Chandler.

Finished size: 89 x 68 in/226 x 175 cm

MATERIALS
All fabrics used in the patchwork top are
45 in/115 cm wide, 100% cotton.

Green flower print and blue: 1¾ yds/1.5 m of each
For the sashing and borders: mauve, 2¼ yds/2 m
**For the sashing corner posts, corner rectangles and
binding:** orange, 1 yd/75 cm
Batting: 2 oz or low loft, 72 x 93 in/185 x 236 cm
Backing: cotton, 72 x 93 in/185 x 236 cm

ALTERNATIVE COLOR SCHEMES

1 Prints in bright colors and black would make an eye-catching quilt for a modern interior; 2 Simple block designs like this will complement a collection of hand-dyed fabrics; 3 Use vintage floral print fabrics teamed with calico for an old-fashioned quilt with nostalgic appeal; 4 The natural colors of earth, sand and rock inspired this combination of colors.

1

2

3

4

CUTTING

1 From the green flower print fabric and the blue fabric, cut ten 14 in/35.5 cm squares each.

> **NOTE**
> You may find it easier to cut one set of squares to the exact size, then cut the partners slightly bigger. Place the pairs right sides together with the accurately cut one on top. Press, then mark and stitch. Now trim the larger squares to size. This will prevent the tendency that these large squares have to skew sideways, making them difficult to fit.

2 From the mauve fabric, cut two strips down the length of the fabric, 10 x 57 in/25.5 x 145 cm wide for the top and bottom borders, and two strips, 8 x 72 in/20.5 x 183 cm wide for the side borders.

3 From the mauve fabric, cut ten strips 2½ in/6.5 cm deep across the width and down the length of the remaining fabric; then sub-cut into 31 rectangles, 13½ in/34.5 cm long for the sashing strips.

4 From the orange fabric, cut one strip, 2½ in/6.5 cm deep, across the width of the fabric; then sub-cut into twelve squares for the "corner posts", i.e. the squares between the sashing strips.

5 From the orange fabric, cut one strip, 8 in/20.5 cm deep across the width of the fabric; then sub-cut into four rectangles 10 in/25.5 cm long for the corner rectangles.

6 From the remaining orange fabric, cut strips, 2½ in/ 6.5 cm deep of sufficient length to go around the outer edges of the quilt for the binding.

STITCHING

1 Place the ten green and blue squares in pairs, right sides together. Draw two diagonal lines on the top fabric of each pair; then pin and stitch ¼ in/0.75 cm away from the marked lines in the pattern illustrated (diagram 1). Trim both squares level if one square was cut larger.

diagram 1

2 Cut across both marked diagonals on each pair; then open out and pin stitch two of the resulting bi-colored triangles together to make one block (diagram 2). Repeat to make twenty blocks.

diagram 2

3 Measure the blocks and check that they are 13½ in/34.5 cm square. If they are larger, trim to size. If they are smaller, trim all to the same size and trim the orange sashing strips to match.

4 Following the quilt assembly plan on page 46, stitch four rows of five blocks with a sashing strip between each. Press the seams towards the blocks.

5 Now pin and stitch three rows of sashing strips together with a corner post between each attached to the short side of the sashing strips. Press seams towards corner posts.

6 Pin and stitch the four rows of blocks together with a long sashing strip between each one, matching points at intersecting corner post squares.

ADDING THE BORDERS

1 Measure the patchwork top from top to bottom through the center and trim two of the mauve border strips to this measurement for the sides. Next measure the patchwork top from side to side through the center and trim the remaining two borders to this measurement for the top and bottom.

2 Pin and stitch the side borders to the patchwork top.

3 Pin and stitch one orange corner rectangle to each end of the two top and bottom mauve border strips; then pin and stitch to the top and bottom of the patchwork top (diagram 3).

diagram 3

FINISHING

1 Spread the backing right side down on a flat surface, then smooth the batting and the patchwork top, right side up, on top. Fasten together with safety pins or baste in a grid.

2 Using the "free motion machine quilting" method, and referring to the photograph as a guide, quilt over the surface. The quilt featured here was quilted on a longarm quilting machine in the "Floral Meander" pattern.

3 Trim the backing and batting level with the edges of the quilt.

4 Join the binding strips with diagonal seams to make a continuous length to fit all around the quilt. Use to bind the edges with a double-fold binding, mitered at the corners.

Sawtooth Fence

Designed by Katharine Guerrier

A strip of sawtooth triangles along the edges of these simple "Rail Fence" blocks give a contemporary look to this traditional favorite. The center panel of sixteen blocks is framed in a border which uses more of the sawtooth triangles. The quilt is made in bright primary colors and uses quick piecing techniques for rapid results. The quilting was done on a longarm quilting machine by Jan Chandler.

Finished size: 55 in/140 cm square

MATERIALS
All fabrics used in the patchwork top are
45 in/115 cm wide, 100% cotton.

For the blocks and borders: 1 yd/1 m each in the
following colors: red, yellow, blue and green
Binding: purple, 20 in/50 cm
Batting: 2 oz or low loft, 60 x 60 in/
152.5 x 152.5 cm
Backing: 100% cotton, 60 x 60 in/152.5 x 152.5 cm

ALTERNATIVE COLOR SCHEMES

1 A combination of plaids and stripes give a homespun effect; 2 Plain colors used together create an Amish-style quilt which shows off the quilting pattern well; 3 Blues teamed with a crisp white are popular in many other forms of decorative art such as Willow Pattern china and Delft floor tiles; 4 Earth colors give a country feel to the quilt, making a homey accent in any interior.

1

2

3

4

CUTTING

1 Remove the selvages from the red and yellow fabrics, then, cutting down the length of the fabric, cut eight strips, 5 in/12.5 cm wide from each color.

2 Cut seven strips, 4 in/10 cm deep across the width of both the green and blue fabrics.

3 From the purple binding fabric, cut strips, $2\frac{1}{2}$ in/6.25 cm deep across the width of the fabric of sufficient length to go around the outer edges of the quilt.

STITCHING

1 Place one red and one yellow strip right sides together and stitch along the long edges, making a $\frac{1}{4}$ in/0.75 cm seam allowance. Press the seams to one side (diagram 1). Repeat with the other seven red and yellow strips.

diagram 1

2 Place one blue and one green strip right sides together and mark off 4 in/10 cm squares; then mark diagonal lines across the squares in a zigzag pattern. Stitch in a zigzag pattern $\frac{1}{4}$ in/0.75 cm away from both sides of the diagonal lines (diagram 2). Cut on the marked vertical and diagonal lines. Open out and press the seams to one side.

diagram 2

3 Repeat with the remaining blue and green strips to make a total of 64 half-square triangle units. Trim each of these bi-colored squares to exactly $3\frac{1}{2}$ in/9 cm, checking that the seam still cuts across the diagonal.

4 Pin and stitch these bi-colored squares together in sets of four to make a sawtooth strip (diagram 3).

diagram 3

ASSEMBLING THE BLOCKS

1 Place one of the sawtooth strips on top of the red/yellow strip, right sides together with the blue fabric against the red. Trim the red/yellow strip even with the sawtooth strip and repeat across the length of the strips. You will then have 16 yellow/red rectangles which are the same length as the sawtooth strips.

2 Pin and stitch the sawtooth strips to the red/yellow rectangles and press (diagram 4). You should have sixteen blocks.

diagram 4

3 Following the quilt assembly diagram on page 52, arrange the blocks in four rows of four blocks each to make the stepped design. Pin and stitch the blocks together in four rows; then stitch the rows together.

ADDING THE BORDERS

1 Using the same technique as you used in step 2 of "Stitching" on the opposite page, make a further 68 bi-colored squares for the border. Stitch these together into two strips of seventeen squares for the bottom and lefthand side of the centre panel, one strip of sixteen squares for the top, and one strip of eighteen squares for the righthand side. Check the quilt assembly diagram for the correct orientation of the seams.

2 Stitch the strip of 16 squares to the top of the panel; then stitch one of the strips of 17 squares to the lefthand side. Next stitch the second strip of 17 squares to the bottom and finally the strip of 18 squares to the righthand side.

FINISHING

1 Spread the backing right side down on a flat surface; then smooth the batting and the patchwork top, right side up, on top. Fasten together with safety pins or baste in a grid.

2 Using the "free motion machine quilting" method, and referring to the photograph as a guide, machine quilt over the surface. The quilt featured here was quilted on a longarm quilting machine in the "Celtic Scroll" pattern.

3 Trim the backing and batting level with the edges of the quilt. Join the binding strips with diagonal seams to make a continuous length to fit all around the quilt. Use to bind the edges with a double-fold binding, mitered at the corners.

Whirligig Quilt

Designed by Dorothy Wood

The success of this quilt depends on accurate cutting and stitching. The plain colored fabrics can be layered together and cut all at once with a rotary cutter. But it is advisable to cut the square patterned fabric in a single layer so that you can see exactly where you are cutting. Depending on the number of plain colors you use, you can create different patterns. Arrange the different colors randomly or in a simple pattern like the diagonal stripes used here.

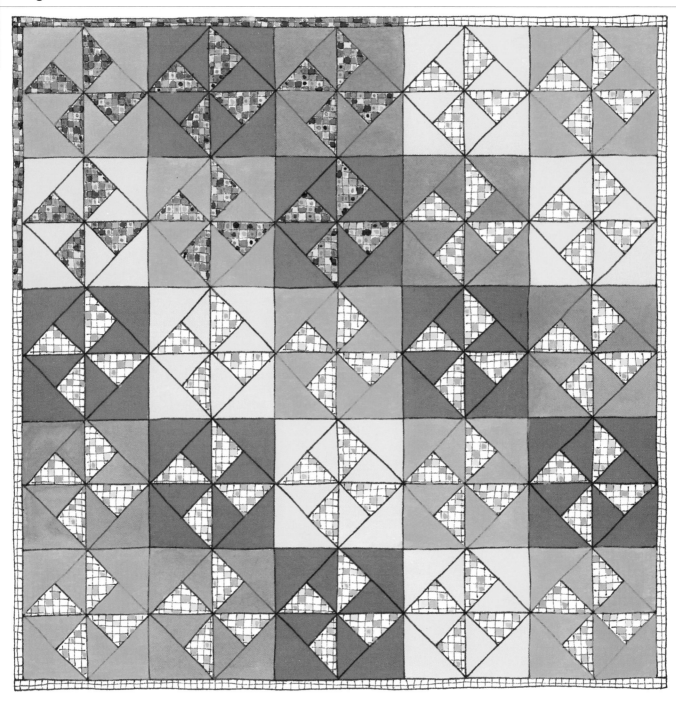

Finished size: 40 x 40 in /102 x 102 cm

MATERIALS
All fabrics used in the patchwork top are
45 in/115 cm wide, 100% cotton.
The backing fabric used is 45in/115cm wide.

Square print: 24 in/60 cm
Yellow, green, fuchsia and orange: 27 in/70 cm each
Backing: 42 x 42 in/107 x 107 cm
Batting: low loft, 42 x 42 in/107 x 107 cm
White sewing thread
Dark blue stranded cotton
Needle

ALTERNATIVE COLOR SCHEMES

1 By stitching the squares together in a slightly different way, you can create a second whirligig pattern; 2 With subtle shades such as this blue and cream check, try to match the creams exactly so that the two fabrics merge together; 3 Choose soft shades of background fabric to coordinate with the subtle stripes; 4 Pink and red are a fun combination. The contrasting patterns work because the pinks and reds are exactly the same color – from the same fabric range.

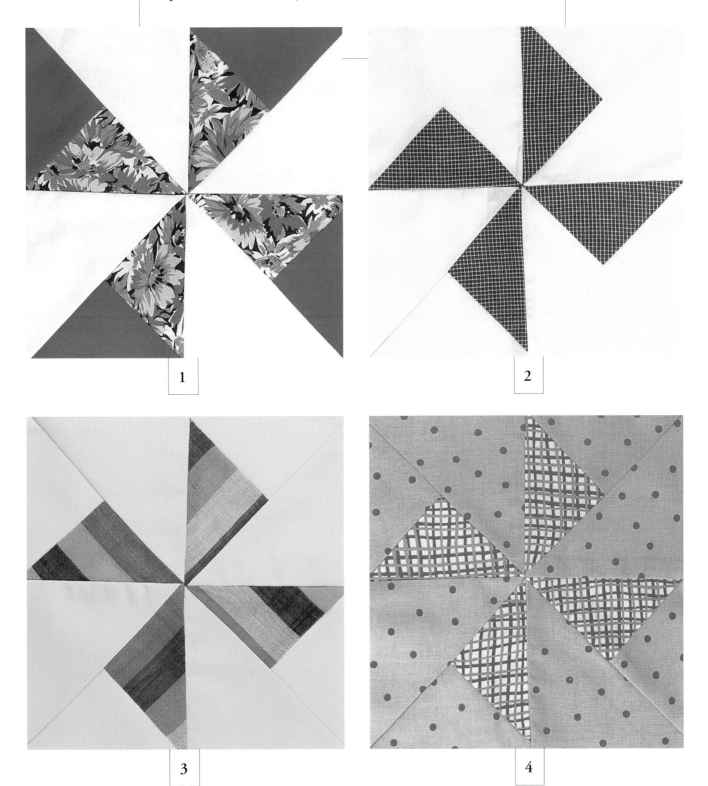

CUTTING

1 From the square print, cut four strips, $2\frac{7}{8}$ in/7.5 cm deep, across the width of the fabric; then cross-cut into fifty $2\frac{7}{8}$ in/7.5 cm squares. Cut the squares in half diagonally.
Cut four strips, $2\frac{3}{8}$ x $17\frac{3}{4}$ in/6 x 45 cm deep, across the width for the binding.

2 Layer the colored fabrics one on top of the other and steam press. Lay on the cutting mat. Cut ten $4\frac{7}{8}$ in/12.5 cm squares, and five $5\frac{1}{4}$ in/13.5 cm squares from all of the colors.

3 Separate the layers and cut four more $4\frac{7}{8}$ in/ 12.5 cm squares from the fuchsia and the orange, and two more from the yellow. Then cut one more $5\frac{1}{4}$ in/13.5 cm square in yellow, and another two in orange and fuchsia.

4 Cut each of the solid colored squares in half diagonally.

STITCHING

NOTE
Follow the directions for pressing the seams carefully so that the seams face in opposite directions when pieces are joined together.

1 Take four of the smaller fuchsia triangles and four of the square print trianges. Arrange as shown in diagram 1.

diagram 1

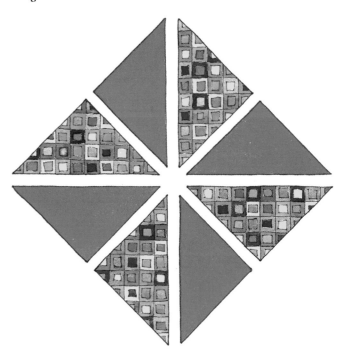

2 Stitch the four square print triangles to the fuchsia triangles using a $\frac{1}{4}$ in/0.75 cm seam to make four larger triangles. Press the seams towards the patterned fabric (diagram 2).

diagram 2

3 Stitch each of the joined triangles to a larger fuchsia triangle along the long edge, using the usual seam allowance. Press the seam towards the plain colored fabric (diagram 3).

diagram 3

4 Arrange the squares to create the whirligig pattern. Pin the top two squares right sides together and stitch with a ¼ in/0.75 cm seam. Press the seam towards the fuchsia fabric. Stitch the bottom two squares together in the same way. Pin and stitch the two units together to finish the block and press the seam to one side.

5 Make all the square blocks in the same way with the remaining fuchsia triangles and the yellow, green and orange triangles, making sure that you press all the seams in the same way as the first block.

6 Following the quilt assembly diagram on page 58, lay out the blocks to form the pattern, with five squares in each of five rows. Check that the seams are all lying vertically. Alternate the direction of the seams in each row by turning the blocks around so that the first row seams face to the left and the next row faces to the right and so on. Pin and stitch the blocks together in rows.

7 Pin the first two rows together, matching the seams carefully, and stitch with a ¼ in/0.75 cm seam. Press the seam downwards.

8 Keep adding the rows one at a time until the patchwork top is complete.

FINISHING

1 Spread the backing right side down on a flat surface, then smooth out the batting and the patchwork top, right side up, on top. Fasten together with safety pins or baste in a grid.

2 Trim the batting and backing fabric to ½ in/ 1.5 cm away from the edge of the patchwork top using a rotary cutter.

3 Pin one of the binding strips down the side of the quilt, right sides together, so that the raw edges are aligned. Stitch with the usual seam allowance.

4 Fold the binding strip to the reverse of the quilt, turn under a ¼ in/0.75 cm hem and slip-stitch to the backing fabric. Trim the ends even with the batting. Repeat to add a binding strip to the opposite side.

5 Pin the remaining two binding strips to the top and bottom of the quilt. Machine stitch as before. Trim the ends of the binding to extend only ¼ in/0.75 cm beyond the quilt. Turn under, even with the edge of the quilt top before folding over and stitching to the reverse side as before.

6 Slip-stitch the corners of the binding neatly.

7 Turn the quilt so that the right side is facing up. To tie the quilt, cut a length of stranded cotton and thread onto a needle. Take a small stitch in the center of the first whirligig block and pull the thread through, leaving a 2 in/5 cm tail. Make a little back stitch and pull the thread through again. Trim to 2 in/5 cm.

8 Stitch a second thread through the center of the whirligig and tie the ends in a reef (square) knot. Trim all thread ends to ½ in /1.5 cm.

A Kiss and A Cuddle

Designed by Sharon Chambers

This oh-so-simple lap quilt made from nostalgic 1930s reproduction fabrics and natural calico is just the thing to warm the heart of someone special. It's the perfect size to cuddle up underneath and there's a kiss sewn right into the middle of it.

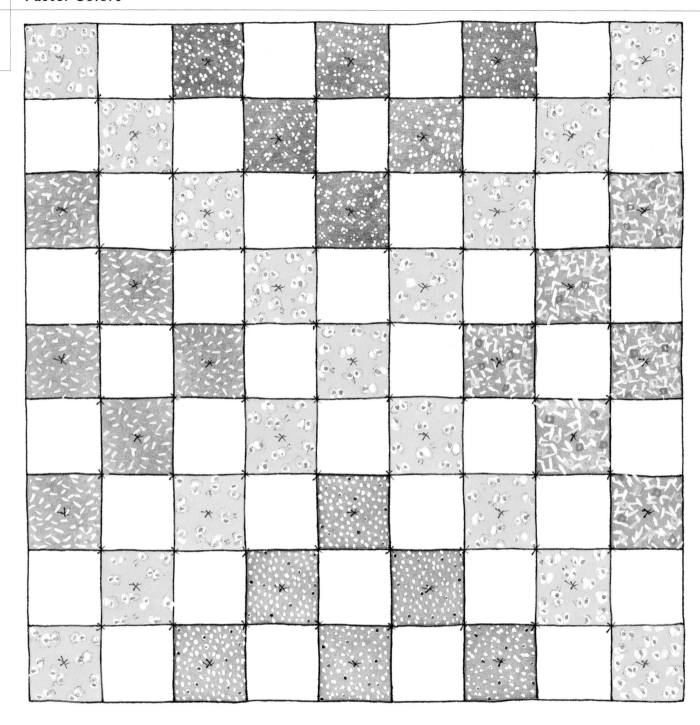

Finished size: 54 x 54 in/135 x 135 cm

MATERIALS

All fabrics used in the quilt top are 45 in/115 cm
wide, 100% cotton.

Main patterned fabric for center "kiss": ⅔ yd/60 cm
Four co-ordinating patterned fabrics: ¼ yd/25 cm of
each

Natural calico for alternate squares: 1½ yds/1.4 m
Backing: 3¼ yds/2.9 m
Batting: 2 oz polyester, 56 x 56 in/140 x 140 cm
Needle: crewel or embroidery needle, or a size three
betweens needle
Stranded embroidery cotton: one skein each of five
colors to match the five patterned fabrics
Coton à broder: one skein no. 16 to match the calico

ALTERNATIVE COLOR SCHEMES

The simplicity of this quilt pattern adapts to so many different possibilities that it is hard to choose. Make it to match a granddaughter's bedroom or in the colors of a grandson's favorite football team. Light or dark, sharp or sweet, it all works. 1 Various pink prints with calico; 2 Red and black plain fabrics with calico; 3 Sharp rich colors with madras plaid; 4 Novelty prints with yellow.

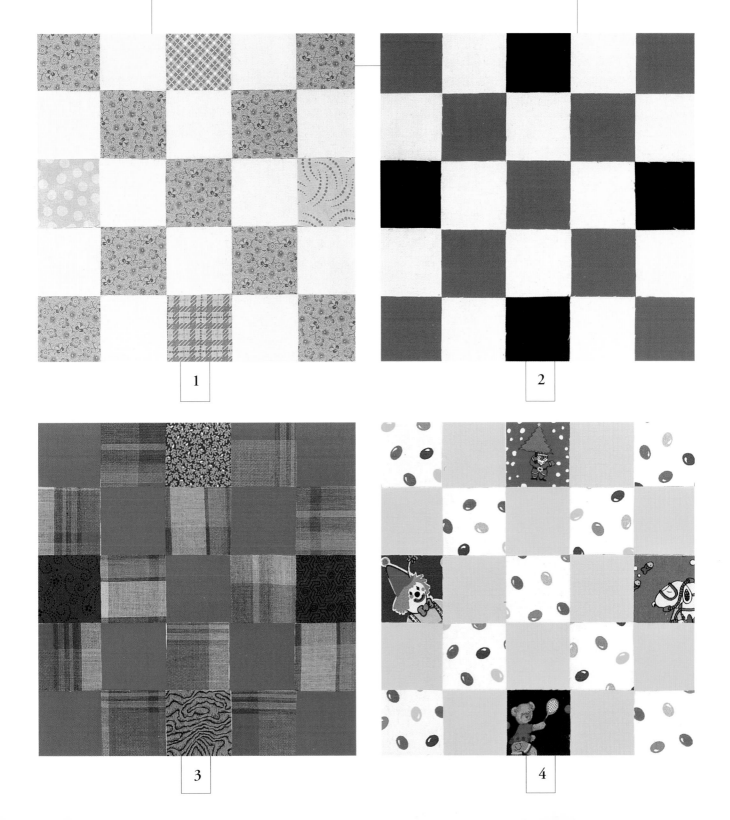

CUTTING

1 From the main patterned fabric, cut three strips, 6½ in/16.5 cm deep, across the width of the fabric. Cross-cut these strips into 6½ in/16.5 cm squares, avoiding the selvages. You should be able to get six squares from each strip, so you will have one left over.

2 From each of the four coordinating patterned fabrics, cut a strip 6½ in/16.5 cm deep, across the width of the fabric. Cross-cut each strip into six 6½ in/16.5 cm squares avoiding the selvages.

3 From the calico, cut seven strips 6½ in/16.5 cm deep across the width of the fabric. Cross-cut these strips into 6½ in/16.5 cm squares avoiding the selvages. You need forty squares, so you will have two left over.

4 Cut the backing fabric into two lengths of 56 in/140 cm each.

STITCHING

1 Following the quilt assembly diagram on page 64, lay out all the fabric squares in their correct places. Stack up the squares for each row so that the first square on the left is at the top of the pile.

2 Beginning with row one and stitching with a ¼ in/0.75 cm seam allowance, stitch the squares together in four pairs (leaving the last square in the row unstitched for the moment).

NOTE Always stack in the same order and pin or tape an identifying letter or number to each row to help you keep the rows in sequence.

3 Stitch the pairs together into two strips of four squares; then stitch these two strips together. Finally, stitch the last square to the end of the row. Set the completed row aside.

4 Stitch the rest of the rows together in exactly the same way. Press all of the seams towards the patterned fabrics. Then when you stitch the rows together, all the short seams will interlock, making it easy to match up seam lines.

5 Pin and stitch the rows together. Press all the long seams in the same direction.

6 Trim the selvages from the backing fabric. With right sides together, seam the two lengths together down the long side, using the usual seam allowance. Press the seam to one side.

FINISHING

NOTE The edges of this quilt are finished without a separate binding, before the tying and quilting are done.

1 Lay the patchwork top over the pieced backing fabric, wrong sides together, with the center seam of the backing aligned with the middle of the patchwork top. Pin the two together to keep them from shifting. Trim off excess backing fabric even with the edges of the patchwork top (diagram 1). Unpin.

diagram 1

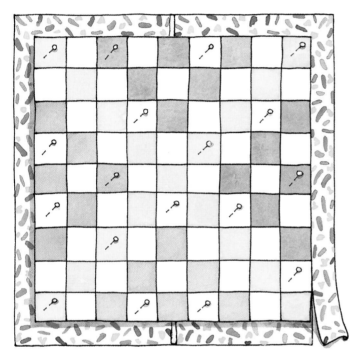

2 Spread out the batting on a smooth flat surface, making sure there are no wrinkles. Place the backing fabric on the batting right side up. Place the quilt top over the backing, right side down, aligning all four edges evenly. Pin with straight pins around the edges to keep them from shifting. Stitch around all four sides with a ¼ in/0.75 cm seam allowance, leaving an opening of about 15 – 18 in/35 – 45 cm on one side for turning. Carefully trim away excess batting across the corners to reduce bulk when turning (diagram 2).

diagram 2

3 Turn quilt right side out, so that the wadding is now sandwiched between the backing and the patchwork top and slip-stitch the opening closed.

4 Smooth out the layers of the quilt, rolling the edges and finger-pressing them so that the seam lies along the edge or just underneath. Pin safety pins along the edges and spaced out over the top to hold everything in place while tying and quilting.

5 Using three strands of embroidery floss, doubled but not knotted, tie as shown in diagram 3. Trim the ends after tying.

diagram 3

6 Mark the quilting pattern in the calico squares as shown in diagram 4 and, using a single strand of coton à broder thread, quilt in large naive style stitches. Finally, stitch a double row of stitches around the outside edge to give a neat finish to the quilt. If you have trouble pulling the knots through to the batting, leave them on the outside or knot one end of the thread to the next. Remember, it's meant to be cuddly, not perfect!

diagram 4

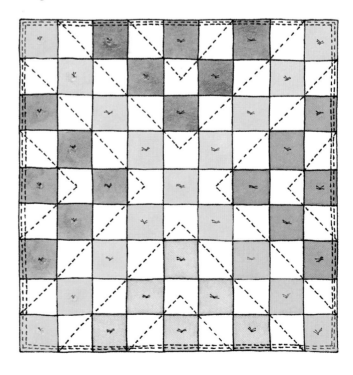

Dotty Cot Quilt

Designed by Rita Whitehorn

This little cot quilt is best suited to a baby from the age of nine months upwards, when he or she can move round more freely and kick off the cover if it becomes too warm. Its mixture of soft pastel blues, pinks, greens, and yellow will suit either a little boy or a little girl.

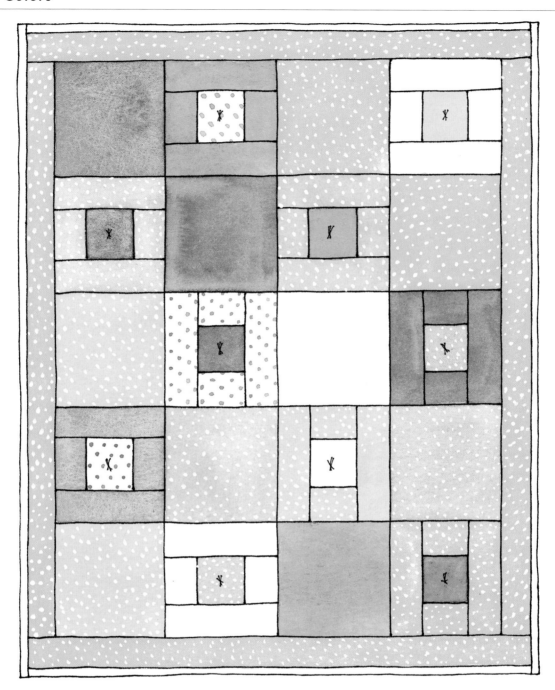

Finished size: 37 x 30 in/86 x 71 cm

MATERIALS
All fabrics used in the quilt top are 45 in/115 cm wide, 100% cotton.

Print fabrics: 9 in/25 cm of each of seven colors. I used pastel small flowery prints in yellow, green, pink and blue, dotty prints in blue and white and pink and white, plus a white-on-white print.
Plain fabrics: 9 in/25 cm of each of four colors. I used pastels in shades of blue, pink, lilac and green to match the prints.

Binding: An extra ½ yd/50 cm of the white-on-white print
Border: An extra ½ yd/50 cm of the green flowery print
Batting: 34 x 41 in/86 x 104 cm
Backing: 34 x 41 in/86 x 104 cm
Template plastic for circle
Marking pencil
Quilting thread
Stranded embroidery cotton or perle

ALTERNATIVE COLOR SCHEMES

Each of these four alternative colorways is based on having a pretty baby's print in the center of the pieced blocks. You can vary the color of the borders around the print to add variety and to pick out the background color for the alternative plain blocks.

1

2

3

4

CUTTING

Follow the quilt assembly diagram on page 70 for the placement of the prints and plain fabrics. Alternatively, make your own color plan before you start.

1 From each of the print and plain fabrics, except the green print, cut one 3¼ x 3¼ in/8 x 8 cm square for the inner squares of the pieced blocks. You need a total of ten small squares.

2 From the print and plain fabrics, except the plain green, cut strips across the width of the fabric, 2¼ in/5.5 cm deep.

3 From the print and plain fabrics cut 10 squares, 6¾ x 6¾ in/16 x 16 cm to alternate with the pieced blocks. You could have a different fabric for each square, but I chose not to use the stronger prints because they would be too dominant. Instead, I cut one each of plain pink, plain blue and plain lilac; one each of pink print, white-on-white and blue print; and two each of green print and yellow print.

4 From the green flowery print, cut 4 strips 2¼ in/5.5 cm deep, across the width of fabric, for the borders.

5 From the white-on-white print, cut 4 strips of fabric 2 in/5 cm deep, across the width of the fabric, for the binding.

STITCHING

1 Following the quilt assembly diagram for the correct matching of fabrics. Place one fabric strip right sides together with one small square, aligning raw edges. Stitch using a ¼ in/0.75 cm seam allowance. Trim the strip level with the square (diagram 1).

diagram 1

2 Repeat to stitch the same strip to the bottom edge of the square and trim (diagram 2a). Press the seams to the darker fabric (diagram 2b).

diagram 2a   *diagram 2b*

3 Repeat as above to stitch a strip to the right side of the block (diagram 3a); then to the left (diagram 3b). This completes the "square within a square" block.

diagram 3a   *diagram 3b*

4 Still following the quilt assembly plan, stitch nine more blocks in the same way.

5 Lay out the blocks alternating with the larger plain squares in five rows of four squares.

6 Stitch the squares in each row together, using a ¼ in/0.75 cm seam allowance; then pin and stitch the rows together, carefully matching seams.

ADDING THE BORDERS

1 Measure the pieced top through the center from top to bottom; then trim two of the border strips to this measurement. Stitch to each side of the top.

2 Measure the pieced top through the center from side to side; then trim two of the border strips to this measurement. Stitch to the top and bottom.

FINISHING

1 Spread the backing right side down on a flat surface; then smooth out the batting and the patchwork top, right side up, on top. Fasten together with safety pins or baste in a grid.

2 Using the template plastic, make a template from the circle given below. Use the template and marking pencil to mark circles in the center of each of the plain squares of the pieced top. Quilt around these circles by hand using large stitches.

3 To add ties to the quilt, lightly mark the center of each inner square of the pieced blocks. Thread a large needle with the embroidery cotton or perlé and insert the needle ¼ in/0.75 cm to the right of the marked center point. Bring needle out about

Template
Actual size

½ in/1.5 cm to the left of the entry point, leaving a "tail" of thread about 3 in/7.5 cm long. Put the needle back into first hole and come back up into the same place as the first exit point. Cut thread about 3 in/7.5 cm from this point. Tie a double knot, but don't pull too tightly. Trim thread to length desired (diagram 4).

diagram 4

4 To bind the quilt, on each of the binding strips fold over ¼ in/0.75 cm of fabric to the wrong side of the fabric and press.

5 Place right side of binding to right side of the quilt top, raw edges to raw edges, and pin tack or baste. Then stitch, using a ¼ in/0.75 cm seam allowance through all the layers. Trim off the excess binding in line with the quilt top.

6 Fold over the binding to the wrong side of the quilt. Slip-stitch in place along the previously pressed up edge, using a matching thread to the binding fabric.

7 Repeat for the left side of the quilt. Add binding strips to the top and bottom in the same way, but turn in a small hem at each end of the strip before folding to the back and hemstitching.

Friends at Heart

Designed by Nikki Foley

Colorful pastels and vibrant pink make this a
beautiful single bed quilt that any girl, no matter
her age, would be delighted to receive as a gift. It
was inspired by sweet peas in a cottage garden.

Finished quilt size: 58½ x 43 in/149 x 109 cm

MATERIALS
All fabrics used in the quilt top are 45 in/115 cm
wide, 100% cotton.

For the blocks: 14 in/35 cm of each of four fabrics –
two pinks and two lilacs

For the inner border and hearts: vibrant pink,
28 in/71 cm
For the outer border: lilac/pink, 15 in/38 cm
Binding: lilac, 10 in/25 cm
Backing: 60 x 45 in/153 x 114 cm
Batting: 60 x 45 in/153 x 114 cm
Machine quilting thread
Fusible webbing

ALTERNATIVE COLOR SCHEMES

Keeping the colors soft and romantic to echo the heart motif, it's still possible to achieve a variety of different effects. 1 Strong purple hearts sit over lilac and cream prints; 2 A checked fabric for the hearts merges well with the floral pale pink and cream fabrics in the four-square blocks; 3 Orange hearts and warm yellows make a sunny color scheme; 4 Strong toned pinks and lilacs produce an ultra-feminine design.

1

2

3

4

CUTTING

1 From the pink and lilac fabrics, first cut off the selvages, then cut into strips, 4½ in/11.5 cm deep, across the width. Because you will be joining the two pink fabrics together and the two lilacs together, they will be referred to as pink **A** and pink **B** and lilac **A** and lilac **B**.

2 From the vibrant pink inner border fabric, cut five strips, 3½ in/9 cm deep, across the width, reserving the remainder for the hearts.

3 From the outer border fabric, cut strips, 3 in/7.5 cm deep, across the width.

4 From the binding fabric, cut strips, 2 in/5 cm deep, across the width.

5 Trace around the heart template given below onto the paper side of the fusible webbing 24 times. Carefully cut around each heart. Place the hearts, paper side up, onto the wrong side of the remaining vibrant pink fabric; then press with a fairly hot iron with the steam off. Cut the hearts out of the fabric, leaving the paper backing on until you are ready to use them.

Template
Actual size

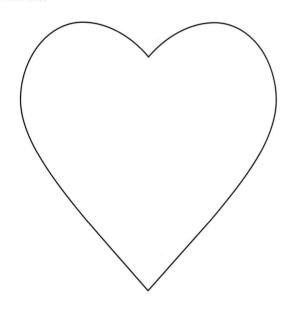

STITCHING

1 To make up the blocks, place a pink A strip right sides together with a pink B strip and stitch, using a ¼ in/0.75 cm seam allowance. Press the seams to one side.

2 Stitch a lilac A strip to a lilac B strip in the same way.

3 Repeat with the remaining two strips of each color; then cut each of these two-color strips into 4½ in/11.5 cm rectangles (diagram 1). You need a total of 24 in pink and 24 in lilac.

diagram 1

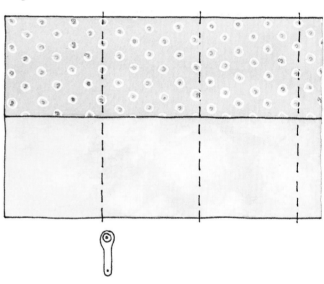

4 Starting with the pink units, place one rectangle on top of another, right sides together, but reversing the colors so that pink A sits on top of pink B. Pin and stitch together to make a four-patch block (diagram 2).

diagram 2

5 Do the same with two lilac rectangles. Repeat to make four-square blocks from all of the remaining rectangles. You should now have 24 blocks altogether – 12 pink and 12 lilac. Press the seams to one side.

6 Following the quilt assembly diagram on page 76, lay out the blocks alternating pink and lilac in four columns, each with six blocks.

7 Pin and stitch the blocks together in rows; then the rows together.

8 Position the hearts in groups of four on the patchwork as shown in diagram 3. When you are happy with the placement, remove the paper backing and iron in place. Take care that the hearts do not move out of place when ironing. Machine stitch around the edge of each heart with a zigzag stitch, using a matching thread.

diagram 3

ADDING THE BORDERS

1 Measure the pieced top through the center from side to side; then make two strips to this length from the vibrant pink inner border strips, joining if necessary. Stitch to the top and bottom of the quilt and press.

2 Measure the pieced top through the center from top to bottom; then join strips of the vibrant pink inner border fabric to this measurement. Stitch to the sides and press.

3 Repeat the measuring and stitching process in steps 1 and 2 to attach the outer border fabric strips to the patchwork top. Press.

FINISHING

1 Spread the backing right side down on a flat surface, then smooth the batting and the patchwork top, right side up, on top. Fasten together with safety pins or baste in a grid.

2 Using a walking foot and decorative stitches, machine quilt as desired. The quilt in the photograph has been quilted with diagonal lines through the four-square blocks and a wavy design along the edges of the inner border.

3 Trim off any excess batting and backing so they are even with the pieced top. Join the binding strips with diagonal seams to make a continuous length to fit all around the quilt. Use to bind the edges with a double-fold binding, mitered at the corners.

NOTE If you don't do the zigzag stitching used to appliqué the hearts all in one go, make a note of the width and length of the stitch used. You may not remember what settings your machine was on next time you come to use it.

Noughts and Crosses

Designed by Sarah Wellfair

This is a simple but highly effective design made up of rail fence blocks and half-square triangles. The similarity of the fabrics used gives an overall pattern to the quilt without emphasizing the patchwork pieces. This quilt could be made bigger by adding more blocks or a wider border. The squares could be made from scraps to make every block a different color scheme.

Finished size: 41 in/103 cm square

MATERIALS
All fabrics used in the quilt top are 45 in/115 cm wide, 100% cotton.

Main fabric for half-square triangles, rail fence block and outer border: cream novelty print, **A**, $1\frac{3}{8}$ yds/1.25 m

For half-square triangles: blue spot, **B**, 10 in/25 cm
For rail fence block: blue cloud pattern, **C**, 10 in/25 cm
For sashing, rail fence block and inner border: green spot, **D**, 20 in/50 cm
Backing: coordinating color, $1\frac{1}{4}$ yds/1 m
Batting: lightweight cotton or polyester, $1\frac{1}{4}$ yds/1 m
Binding: cream, 20 in/50 cm

ALTERNATIVE COLOR SCHEMES

1 A selection of Christmas fabrics in traditional colors looks really festive; 2 A range of autumn reds, golds and purples makes a warm and comforting quilt; 3 A variety of different blue prints produces a harmonious color scheme; 4 Fabrics with a check or a plaid pattern work well with matching floral fabrics interspersed with some plain.

1

2

3

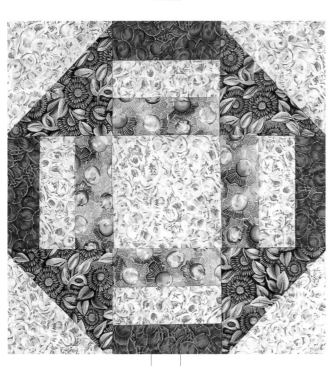

4

CUTTING

1 From fabric **A,** cut the following:
two strips, $1\frac{7}{8}$ x 44 in/5 x 114 cm;
eight squares, $5\frac{1}{2}$ in/14.5 cm;
four squares, $4\frac{5}{8}$ in/12 cm;
one square, $2\frac{1}{2}$ in/6.5 cm;
two strips, $4\frac{1}{2}$ x $40\frac{1}{4}$ in/11.5 x 101 cm;
two strips, $4\frac{1}{2}$ x $31\frac{3}{4}$ in/11.5 x 79.5 cm.

2 From fabric **B,** cut eight squares, $5\frac{1}{2}$ in/14.5 cm.

3 From fabric **C,** cut two strips, $1\frac{7}{8}$ x 44 in/
5 x 114 cm.

4 From fabric **D,** cut the following:
two strips, $1\frac{7}{8}$ x 44 in/5 x 114 cm;
four strips, $2\frac{1}{2}$ x $12\frac{7}{8}$ in/6.5 x 33 cm;
two strips, $2\frac{1}{2}$ x $27\frac{1}{4}$ in/6.5 x 68 cm;
two strips, $2\frac{1}{2}$ x $31\frac{3}{4}$ in/6.5 x 79.5 cm.

NOTE The block is made up of four half-square triangles, four rail fence blocks and one plain square. It will help with the assembly if you label each of the different fabrics A to D, as shown in diagram 1.

diagram 1

STITCHING

1 Take one $1\frac{7}{8}$ in/5 cm strip of **A** and one $1\frac{7}{8}$ in/5 cm strip of **C,** place right sides together and stitch down one long side using a $\frac{1}{4}$ in/0.75 cm seam. Do the same to the remaining two strips of the same color.

2 Take the two **D** $1\frac{7}{8}$ in/5 cm wide strips and stitch to the other side of the cream strips with the same seam allowance. Press the seams towards the darker fabric.

3 The strips should now be approx $4\frac{5}{8}$ in/12 cm wide. Using a rotary cutter and ruler, cross-cut the strips into $4\frac{5}{8}$ in/12 cm squares – you will need 16 squares in total (diagram 2).

diagram 2

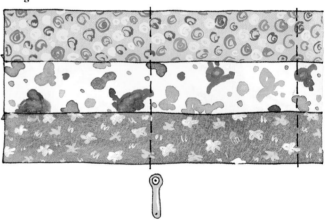

4 Take one **A** $5\frac{1}{2}$ in/14.5 cm square and place right sides together with one **B** $5\frac{1}{2}$ in/14.5 cm square. Repeat with the remaining seven **A** and **B** squares. With the cream fabric uppermost, pencil draw a line diagonally from corner to corner.

5 Stitch $\frac{1}{4}$ in/0.75 cm on either side of the marked line on all eight squares (diagram 3).

diagram 3

6 Cut squares in half along the marked line. Open and press the seams towards the darker fabric. You should now have 16 squares of half-square triangles.

7 Following the block layout in diagram 1, lay out the pieced squares. Using the usual seam allowance, stitch together first in rows; then stitch the rows together, being careful to match seams as you go. Stitch all four blocks the same way.

8 Take two of the $2\frac{1}{2}$ x $12\frac{7}{8}$ in/6.5 x 33 cm sashing strips, **D**, and stitch one $2\frac{1}{2}$ in/6.5 cm square to the short end of one strip. Then stitch the other sashing strip to the opposite side of the square. Press the seams towards the sashing strips (diagram 4).

diagram 4

9 Take the other two sashing strips and stitch one between each pair of blocks. Press the seams towards the sashing (diagram 5).

diagram 5

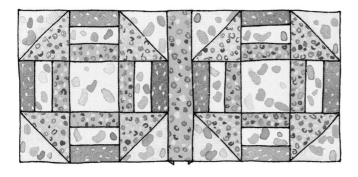

10 Stitch the sashing strip made in step 8 between the two units made in step 9.

ADDING THE BORDERS

1 Take two $27\frac{1}{4}$ in/68 cm inner border strips, **D**, and pin and stitch one to the top edge and one to the bottom edge of the patchwork.

2 Take the remaining two $31\frac{3}{4}$ in/79.5 cm inner border strips, **D**, and pin and stitch to the sides.

3 Take the two $31\frac{3}{4}$ in/79.5 cm outer border strips, **A**, and stitch to the top and bottom of the quilt.

4 Take the remaining two $40\frac{1}{4}$ in/101 cm outer border strips, **A**, and stitch to the sides of the quilt.

FINISHING

1 Measure the patchwork top and give it a final pressing.

2 Cut the batting and backing 2 in/5 cm bigger all around than the finished quilt size.

3 Spread the backing right side down on a flat surface; then smooth the batting and the patchwork top, right side up, on top. Fasten together with safety pins or baste in a grid.

4 Machine quilt as desired. I have random quilted the center and quilted free motion random hearts in the border.

5 Trim the excess batting and backing even with the patchwork top.

6 Cut the binding fabric into 3 in/7.5 cm strips across the width of the fabric. Fold in half lengthwise and press.

7 Measure the quilt through the center from top to bottom and cut two of the binding strips to this length. Pin one strip to the side of the quilt, matching raw edges. Stitch approximately $\frac{1}{2}$ in/1.5 cm in from the edge. Fold over to the back of the quilt, turn under a hem and slip-stitch down. Do the same on the opposite side of the quilt with the remaining strip.

8 Measure the quilt through the center from side to side and add $1\frac{1}{2}$ in/4 cm to this for turning. Cut two more binding strips to this length. Stitch to the top and bottom of the quilt, turning in a short hem at either end before folding to the back. Turn under a hem and slip-stitch to the backing.

Pretty Pinwheels

Designed by Alison Wood

There are many different traditional quilt blocks which can be made from half-square triangles such as these. But the pinwheel is a simple and striking setting. Spacing the pinwheels with alternate plain squares gives an uncluttered look and, for lovers of hand quilting, there is plenty of scope for embellishment. The quilt can be made with treasured scraps or with just two contrasting fabrics for a strong graphic look. The quilt shown uses 17 fabrics based on a collection of 10 coordinating florals with the addition of some crisp ginghams and pastel marble fabrics. The width means that it can be inexpensively backed with 60 in/154 cm-wide calico.

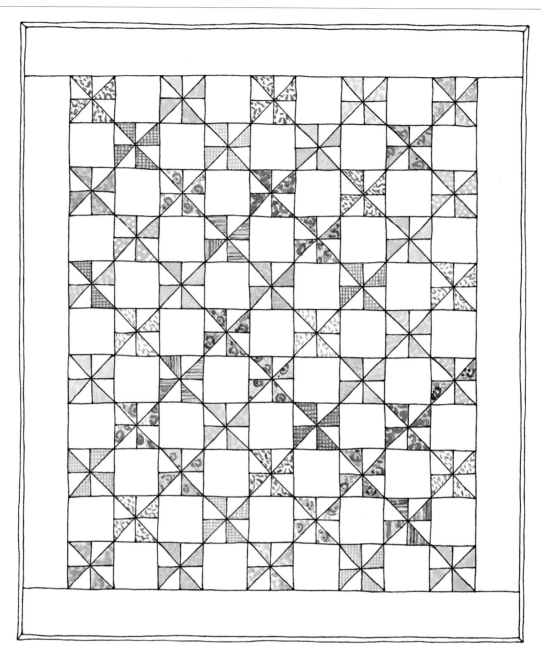

Finished size: 67 x 55 in/170 x 140 cm

MATERIALS

The white calico used in the quilt top is 60 in/154 cm wide. An alternative quantity is given for 45 in/115 cm-wide background fabric.

Pinwheels: main fabric, $\frac{3}{4}$ yd/75 cm, 45 in/115 cm wide. If using scraps, a minimum of two $3\frac{1}{8}$ in/8 cm squares are needed for each pinwheel block, and 100 squares are needed altogether. A fat eighth of a yard or meter should yield 18 x $3\frac{1}{8}$ in/8 cm squares; a fat quarter should yield 36 squares.

Background pinwheel fabric: calico, $\frac{2}{3}$ yd/60 cm, 60 in/154 cm wide OR $\frac{3}{4}$ yd/75 cm, 45 in/115 cm wide

Plain alternate squares: calico, $\frac{7}{8}$ yd/75 cm, 60 in/154 cm wide OR 1 yd/1 m, 45 in/115 cm wide

Borders: calico, $\frac{2}{3}$ yd/60 cm, 60 in/154 cm wide OR 1 yd/1 m, 45 in/115 cm wide

Binding: $\frac{1}{2}$ yd/50 cm or use scraps

Backing: calico, 2 yds/2 m, 60 in/154 cm wide OR 4 yds/3.5 m, 45 in/115 cm-wide fabric cut in half and joined with the seam running horizontally

Batting: approx. 72 x 92 in/183 x 234 cm (twin or single size). Cotton or 80:20 cotton/polyester mix is more suitable for machine quilting. For hand quilting use either cotton/cotton blend or 2 oz polyester.

Medium lead pencil or quilt marking pencil

Hera marker (optional)

ALTERNATIVE COLOR SCHEMES

1 Rainbow stripes and a purple print make an eye-catching contemporary design – make sure the stripes always run parallel to one of the seams; 2 The strong contrast of indigo and white is highly effective; 3 Soft country floral and pastel polka dots make a restful quilt; 4 Plaids and dots in bright colors make a zingy colorway for a child's room.

1

2

3

4

CUTTING

1 From the fabric or fabrics chosen for the pin-wheels, cut strips $3\frac{1}{8}$ in/8 cm deep, across the width. Cross-cut the strips into $3\frac{1}{8}$ in/8 cm squares. You will need 100 squares. Put these to one side.

2 From the background fabric, cut 100 x $3\frac{1}{8}$ in/8 cm squares in the same way.

3 For the plain alternate squares, cut 5 in/12.5 cm strips and cross-cut into 5 in/12.5 cm squares. You will need 49 squares.

NOTE You may wish to delay cutting the plain alternate blocks (step 3) until you have pieced the pinwheel blocks. Seam allowance and stitching accuracy varies, and you may find that your completed blocks are slightly more or slightly less than 5 in/12.5 cm. The alternate blocks must be exactly the same size as the pinwheel blocks if they are to fit together easily and well.

4 From the border fabric, if it is 60 in/154 cm wide, cut four 5 in/12.5 cm strips; if 45 in/115 cm wide, cut six strips of the same depth and set aside.

5 Cut the binding fabric into strips, $2\frac{1}{2}$ in/6 cm deep, across the width of the fabric.

STITCHING

1 Draw a diagonal line across the wrong side of each of the 100 background squares with a marking pencil and ruler.

2 Take one pinwheel square and one background square and place right sides together. Stitch a seam line $\frac{1}{4}$ in/0.75 cm away from and on each side of the drawn diagonal line (diagram 1). Repeat with the remaining 99 squares. Use the chain-piecing method to save time and thread.

diagram 1

3 Cut the threads between the squares. Press each stitched pair of squares flat to set the seams; then cut along the drawn diagonal line.

4 Press each unit open with the seam allowance towards the darker fabric. Trim off the small "ears" of fabric which extend beyond the square.

5 Lay out four squares as shown in diagram 2. You will see that pinwheel blocks are directional and can spin right or left depending how you place the units. Decide which way you want them to spin; then be consistent.

diagram 2

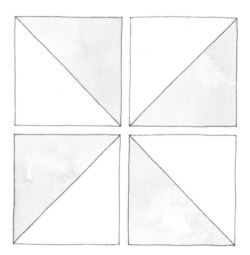

6 Pick up two of the units from the pinwheel and place one on top of the other, right sides together. Carefully match the edge you will stitch to join the units and make sure that the diagonal seams of both units butt together accurately. You can feel the fit with your fingertips. This is where careful attention to always pressing in the same direction really pays off.

7 Stitch along the righthand edge of the pair; then pick up the remaining pair of units from that pinwheel, snuggle the seam allowances together and stitch the seam. If you are not sure that you are stitching along the correct edge, pin the seam first and open out the pair, checking against your layout.

8 Chain-piece all the remaining pinwheel units in pairs. Don't snip the thread between the pairs because you may find that this little twist of thread will help to keep each pinwheel's pieces together (diagram 3).

diagram 3

9 Join each pair of half-pinwheels to the other. Stitch along the long edge, taking particular care over the crossing point in the center of the pinwheel (diagram 4). Press the seam open to reduce bulk in the center of the block.

diagram 4

NOTE It is worth taking time to match points in the center of the block, but if you are not entirely happy with the end result you can sew a decorative button in the center of the pinwheel (but not on quilts for babies or young children).

10 Lay the completed blocks on the floor, alternating with the plain squares, following the quilt assembly plan on page 88. Note that each even numbered row starts and finishes with a plain square, whereas the odd numbered rows begin and end with a pinwheel.

11 Pin and stitch the blocks into 11 rows, each containing 9 blocks. Press the rows carefully. If you press the seam allowances between the blocks in opposite directions for alternate rows you will be able to butt them together when joining the rows. That gives a neat fit with sharp points where the pinwheels meet.

12 Pin and stitch the rows together and press the top lightly.

ADDING THE BORDERS

1 Measure the patchwork top through the center from top to bottom and cut both the side borders to this length. You may need to join strips to have pieces that are long enough. Pin and stitch to the sides of the patchwork. Press the seam allowance towards the borders.

2 Measure the patchwork top through the center from side to side and cut both the top and bottom borders to this length. Pin and stitch to the top and bottom of the patchwork. Press as before.

FINISHING

1 Measure the completed patchwork top and, if necessary, cut and piece backing to fit with at least 2 in/5 cm extra on all sides. If you are joining the backing, don't forget to cut off the selvages since these are very tightly woven and can cause distortion in the quilt. Press the seam open.

2 Spread the backing right side down on a flat surface; then smooth the batting and the patchwork top, right side up, on top. Fasten together with safety pins or baste in a grid.

3 Mark the top with the desired quilting design. The quilt shown was marked in long diagonal lines through the plain squares and also through the diagonals of the pinwheels with a plastic tool called a Hera marker and a long ruler. The marker makes an indentation in the layered quilt which shows up well on light colored fabric. Machine quilt along the marked lines.

4 Join the binding strips with diagonal seams to make a continuous length to fit all round the quilt. Use to bind the edges with a double-fold binding, mitered at the corners.

Sherbet Twist

Designed by Sharon Chambers

Mouth-watering colors, a broderie anglaise frill and a scattering of mother-of-pearl buttons make this lap quilt the perfect treat for a sweet little girl. The plain white strips make assembly quick and easy, and the quilt sandwich is simply secured with buttons.

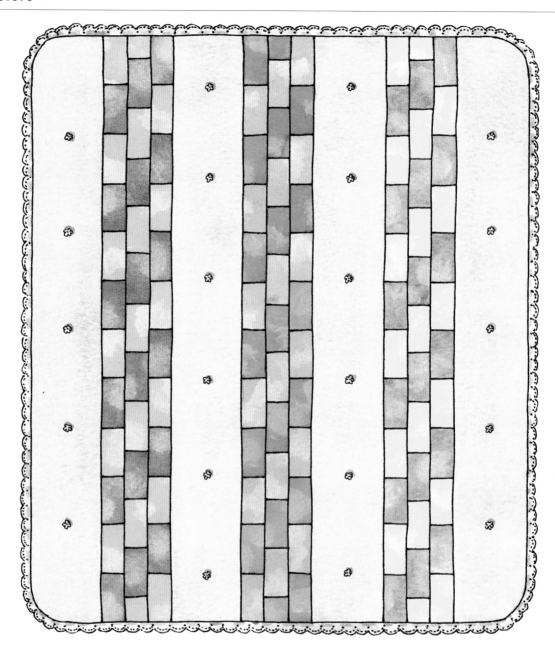

Finished size: 60 x 52½ in/144 x 126 cm

MATERIALS

All fabrics used in the quilt top are 45 in/115 cm
wide, 100% cotton.
The backing fabric is 60 in /150 cm wide.

For the sherbet twist strips: ⅓ yd/30 cm of each of
six different pastel colorways of the same fabric
design
Vertical sashing: white-on-white patterned fabric,
1¾ yds/1.6 m
Marking pencil
Pre-gathered broderie anglaise frill to edge quilt:
6½ yds/5.75 m

Buttons: 22 small mother-of-pearl
Backing: bleached calico, 1¾ yds/1.6 m
Batting: soft 2 oz polyester, 56½ x 64 in/
136 x 154 cm
Quilting thread: white

NOTE

Because I wanted a puffy eiderdown
effect, I used a double layer of 2 oz
batting, which means using two pieces of
the size given.

ALTERNATIVE COLOR SCHEMES

The simplicity of this pattern allows for any favorite color scheme a little girl could wish for: 1 Lilacs and pinks; 2 Minty greens with apricot; 3 Bright fruit sorbet combinations; 4 Lots of different floral prints.

1

2

3

4

diagram 1

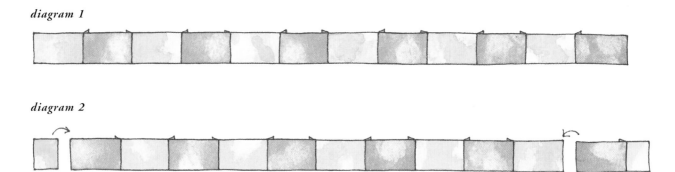

diagram 2

CUTTING

Before you cut your pastel fabrics, decide how to group them. There are three pairs of fabrics. Within each pair there is a dominant color from which you will cut 18 rectangles, and a secondary fabric from which you will cut 17 rectangles and two half-rectangles.

1 From each of the pastel fabrics, cut three strips, 3 in/7.5 cm deep, across the whole width of the fabric.

2 Divide your fabrics into your chosen pairs. From the dominant fabric of the first pair cross-cut the strips into 3 x 5½ in/7.5 x 13.5 cm rectangles. Each strip yields seven, but you only need 18. From your secondary fabric cross-cut two of the strips into 3 x 5½ in/7.5 x 13.5 cm rectangles to yield 14 rectangles. From the third strip cut three more rectangles and two half-rectangles 3 x 3 in/7.5 x 7.5 cm. Stack all of these in two piles and set aside.

3 Repeat step 2 for the other two pairs of pastels.

4 From the white-on-white patterned fabric cut four strips, 8 in/19.5 cm wide down the length of the fabric, i.e. parallel to but not including the selvages.

STITCHING

1 Using your first pair of pastel fabrics, place one secondary fabric rectangle right sides together with a dominant fabric rectangle. Stitch along a short side, using a ¼ in/0.75 cm seam allowance. Continue in this fashion until you have 17 pairs of rectangles stitched together.

2 Divide these into two stacks of six and one stack of five. Place the remaining rectangle and two half-rectangles with the stack of five and set aside.

3 From the first stack of six, stitch the pairs together, alternating the colors until you have a strip of 17 rectangles (diagram 1). Do the same for the second stack of six.

4 Stitch the last stack together into a strip of 10 rectangles. Stitch one of the half-rectangles to the remaining full-sized one; then add it to one end of the strip, keeping the alternate colors in their correct sequence (diagram 2). Add the remaining half-rectangle to the other end of the strip.

5 Following the quilt assembly diagram on page 94, lay the three strips out so you can check that they are in the correct order. Press the seams towards the darker fabric. Pin and stitch the first and second strips together.

6 Add the third strip in the same way. Press the long seams towards the center strip.

7 Stitch the second and third sets of fabric in the same way and press. You may find that there is a slight variation in length between the three sets of strips. If so, measure and trim them to the same length. Use this trimmed measurement to trim the four sashing strips to the correct size.

8 Pin one sashing strip to one pieced strip with right sides together. Stitch with a ¼ in/0.75 cm seam allowance.

9 Pin and stitch the remaining four sashing strips in the same way. Press the seams towards the pieced strips.

ADDING THE FRILL

1 To round off the corners of the pieced top, use a saucer to mark the curve. Lay it on the corner so that the edge is just touching both sides, hold it firmly in place and draw around it with a marking pencil. Trim along the line (diagram 3). Repeat for all four corners.

diagram 3

2 To add the frill, start about three-quarters of the way down the righthand side. Pin the broderie anglaise to the edge of the pieced top, right sides together, with the frill facing towards the center of the quilt and the pre-gathered edge aligned with the edge of the quilt (diagram 4).

diagram 4

3 Overlap the end by about 1 in/2.5 cm. Unpin about 6 in/15 cm at the beginning of the frill and start stitching at that point, using a ¼ in /0.75 cm seam allowance. Stitch all around the quilt to about 6 in/15 cm from the end. Stop and break the thread.

4 Overlap the ends of the frill by about 1 in/2.5 cm and trim off the excess. Pin the short ends of the frill with right sides together. Stitch. Trim one side of the seam allowance to ¼ in/0.75 cm and fold the other side over it. Slip-stitch the folded side down (diagram 5). Now that the ends are joined you can finish stitching the frill in place.

diagram 5

FINISHING

1 Trim your backing fabric to the same size as the quilt top.

2 If you are using 2 oz batting doubled over, make sure that both layers are smooth. Lay the batting on a flat surface. Place the backing fabric on the batting right side up. Place the quilt on top with the right side down. Pin all three layers together, making sure that the frill is tucked inside so it doesn't get caught in the seam. Stitch around all four sides, leaving an opening of about 15 in/40 cm on the bottom edge for turning. Turn the quilt right side out and slip-stitch the opening closed behind the frill. Smooth the quilt out evenly and pin to hold it in place.

3 Hand quilt in-the-ditch down the long seams. You will probably find that you have to take larger stitches because of the thicker batting.

4 Finally, stitch the buttons in place using the quilt assembly diagram as a guide.

Tulip Field

Designed by Dorothy Wood

You can use any patterned fabric to make this quilt, but to create a cohesive design choose plain fabrics in the exact shade of some of the colors within the patterned fabric. Instead of quilting by hand or machine, simply "tie" the quilt together at regular intervals with buttons. I chose rustic buttons that have a similar shade to one of the colors in the patterned fabric. They contrast with the plain fabrics but their tone is still in keeping with the quilt top as a whole.

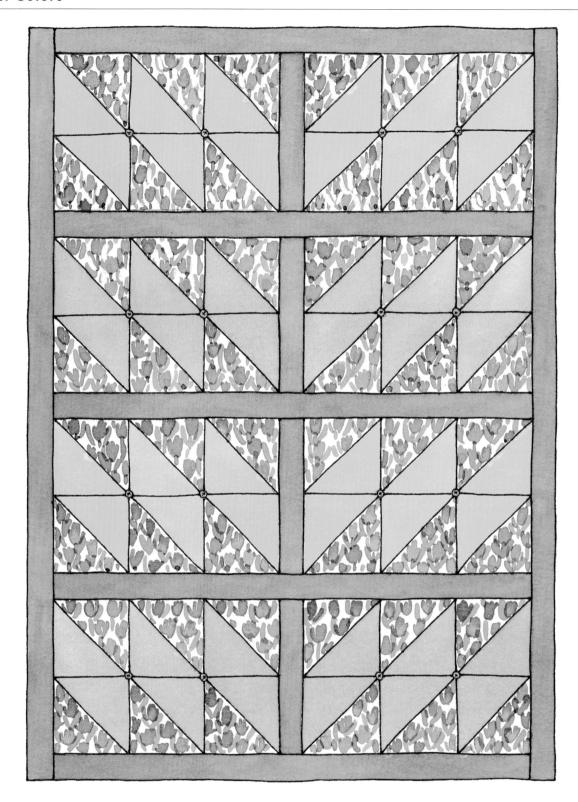

Finished size: 56 x 40 in /142 x 102 cm

MATERIALS

All fabrics used in the quilt top are 45 in/115 cm wide, 100% cotton.

The backing fabric is 59 in /150 cm wide.

Tulip print: 1 yd/1 m

For the triangles: yellow and green, 18 in/50 cm

For the sashing and binding: pink, 1³⁄₄ yds/1.60 m

Backing: 40 x 56 in /102 x 142 cm

Batting: low loft, 40 x 56 in/102 x 142 cm

White sewing thread

16 buttons

Deep pink sewing thread

Needle

ALTERNATIVE COLOR SCHEMES

1 This bright flower fabric has a pale blue background color that can be used for the binding and sashing – the paler color softens the effect and pulls the fabrics together; 2 The classic blue and off-white combination makes a subtle country-style quilt ideal for a guest bedroom; 3 This striking fruit print makes a bright, bold quilt – use the yellow in the print as the alternative to the lime green in the blocks; 4 The paisley pattern combined with a spot fabric in matching colors gives an offbeat look for a young girl's bedroom.

1

2

3

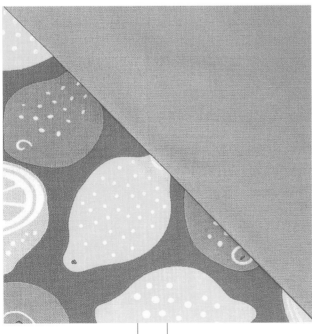

4

CUTTING

1 From the tulip print, cut twenty-four 6⅞ in/ 17.5 cm squares, ensuring that the tulips all face in the same direction. Cut 12 of the squares in half diagonally from top left to bottom right, and the other 12 diagonally from top right to bottom left.

2 From both the yellow and the green fabrics, cut twelve 6⅞ in/17.5 cm squares. Cut each square in half diagonally.

3 From the pink fabric, cut four 12¼ x 2½ in/31 x 6.5 cm strips and three 37 x 2½ in/94 x 6.5 cm strips for the sashing; cut two 37 x 4½ in/94 x 11.5 cm strips and two 60 x 4½ in/152.5 x 11.5 cm strips, joining as necessary, for the binding.

STITCHING

1 Arrange the first block of yellow and tulip print triangles as shown in diagram 1. Stitch the triangles in pairs, using a ¼ in/0.75 cm seam allowance to make six squares. Press the seams towards the tulip print.

diagram 1

2 Stitch the top row of three squares together with ¼ in/0.75 cm seams and press the seams to the left. Stitch the bottom row of squares together and press the seams to the right.

3 Pin the two rows right sides together matching the seams. Stitch together with ¼ in/0.75 cm seams. Press the seams downwards.

4 Stitch the green and tulip print blocks in the same way, laying the triangles out as shown in diagram 2 to create the blocks before stitching so that no mistakes are made.

diagram 2

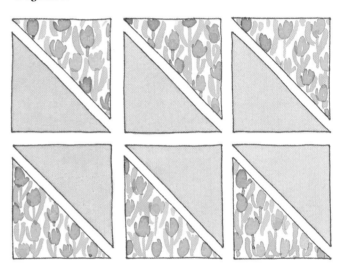

5 Repeat to stitch another block of yellow and tulip print squares and another of green and tulip print following the quilt assembly diagram on page 100. Then reverse the layout of the triangles (following the quilt assembly diagram) and stitch two more blocks of yellow and tulip print, plus two more of green and tulip print squares. Lay out the eight blocks as shown in the quilt assembly diagram.

6 Pin one of the short 12¼ x 2½ in/31 x 6.5 cm lengths of sashing right sides together along the right-hand side of the top lefthand yellow panel. Stitch with a ¼ in/0.75 cm seam and press away from the sashing. Pin the top righthand yellow panel to the other side of the sashing and stitch and press as before (diagram 3).

diagram 3

7 Stitch the two green panels together with a short strip of sashing in the same way; then the remaining panels. Press the seams towards the pieced blocks.

8 Fold the three middle-sized 37 x $2\frac{1}{2}$ in/94 x 6.5 cm strips of sashing in half to find the mid-point. Pin one strip along the bottom of the top yellow panel, right sides together and matching the mid-point to the center of the short sashing strip. Stitch with a $\frac{1}{4}$ in/0.75 cm seam.

9 Pin and stitch the first green panel to the other side of the sashing strip. Press the seams towards the blocks.

10 Work down the quilt, adding sashing strips between the panels to create the pieced top as shown in the quilt assembly diagram.

11 Using $\frac{1}{4}$ in/0.75 cm seams, pin and stitch the two shorter binding strips across the top and bottom of the pieced top. Press the seams towards the blocks.

12 Pin and stitch the longer binding strips down each side of the pieced top. Press the seams towards the quilt.

FINISHING

1 Lay out the pieced top right side down. Place the batting on top and smooth it out, checking that there is the same amount of pink fabric border showing all around. Press the backing fabric and lay on top of the batting right side up. Tack around the edge.

2 Fold under $\frac{1}{4}$ in/0.75 cm of the binding all around the pieced top and finger press to hold it in position. At the sides fold the binding over the batting and backing fabric and pin. Fold over the binding along the top and bottom edges and pin.

3 Slip-stitch the corners and hem the binding to the backing fabric (diagram 4). Turn the quilt over. Pin at the point between the colored blocks where the buttons will be stitched.

diagram 4

4 Using a deep pink thread, sew a button where you have inserted the pins. Sew the threads to make a cross pattern on the button. Press the binding very gently to finish the quilt.

Matrix Quilt

Designed by Gail Smith

This quilt is very simple to make (it took approximately 12 hours), and with its contrasting sashing and borders, it's an ideal design to showcase your favorite fabrics. In this example, a collection of blue and green fabrics reminds us of the colors of the sea. It is framed perfectly by the dark blue sashing and borders.

Finished size: 62 x 42 in/155 x 107 cm

MATERIALS
All fabrics used in the quilt top are 45 in/115 cm wide, 100% cotton.

For center squares and middle border: 6 in/15 cm across the width of at least 5 different blue and blue/green fabrics. These should be of approximately the same value, i.e. light or medium and preferably not too dark, because there needs to be a good contrast with the sashing fabric. (Fossil fern fabrics are ideal; also tone-on-tone fabrics.)

For middle border: 12 in/30 cm in addition to one of the five fabrics above, cut across the width
For inner and outer borders and the sashing: dark blue, 2¼ yds/2 m. This should be darker than the fabric for the squares.
Binding: 7½ in/19 cm, cut across the width. (We chose one of the fabrics used for the center squares.)
Backing: 100% cotton or sheeting, 66 x 46 in/ 165 x 117 cm
Batting: either 2 oz polyester or a cotton alternative, 66 x 46 in/165 x 117 cm
Machine thread: preferably cotton, to match
Variegated machine quilting thread (optional)

ALTERNATIVE COLOR SCHEMES

1 Novelty fabrics for the center square with dark sashing makes an equally bold design; 2 African fabric with coordinating sashing makes a great quilt for an animal lover; 3 Brown and gold fabrics give a classic look; 4 Pink and purple squares with lilac sashing produce a pretty, feminine design.

1

2

3

4

CUTTING

NOTE Remove selvage from fabric prior to starting. The seam allowance is ¼ in/0.75 cm throughout.

1 From the five strips for the center squares, cut 40 squares measuring 6 x 6 in/15 x15 cm.

2 From the dark blue, cut four strips, 2 in/5 cm deep, across the width for the horizontal sashing strips.

3 From the remaining dark blue, cut eight strips, 2 in/5 cm wide and 54 in/137 cm long down the length of the fabric. Four will be used for the vertical sashing and four for the inner borders. Cut four strips, 2½ in/6 cm wide and 64 in/163 cm long down the length of the fabric for the outer borders.

NOTE You may wish to cut the outer border strips after construction of the center panel, as measurements may vary slightly.

4 From the middle border fabric, cut five strips, 1¼ in/3 cm deep, across the width for the binding, totaling at least 200 in/508 cm altogether (to be joined together later).

5 Cut the binding fabric into strips, 1½ in/4 cm deep, across the width of the fabric.

STITCHING

1 Lay out the 40 squares in five rows, each with eight squares across. The arrangement of the colors is not important at this stage. Place the four horizontal sashing strips in between.

2 To attach the sashing to the bottom of each square work as follows: lay a sashing strip right side up on your sewing machine. Then place a 6 in/15 cm square, right side down on top of the sashing, aligning the raw edges. Stitch it to the sashing. Do not break

the thread or cut the sashing fabric, but add another square right side down and stitch. Keep on going until you have attached seven squares in this way (diagram 1). You do not need to stitch on the remaining eighth square at this stage.

diagram 1

3 Repeat step 2 to attach the squares in the next four rows in the same way. You should have 5 spare squares.

4 Trim the sashing even with the squares and press the resulting units open with the seams pressed towards the sashing (diagram 2). Following the quilt assembly diagram on page 106, lay out the units in columns with the sashing strips at the bottom, moving the squares until you are happy with the layout. Take care not to have two squares of the same color close to each other. Balance the colors across the

diagram 2

quilt. Place a spare square at the bottom of each column. You may need to number them by pinning on strips of paper (column 1 unit 1, for example) to ensure they are stitched together in the same layout.

5 Starting at the top of column 1, stitch the sashing of unit 1 to the top of the square below it, and carry on down the first column. When you get to the bottom, attach the spare square. Repeat four times. You should now have five columns, each column starting and ending in a square. Press your work.

6 You are now ready to add the vertical sashing strips in between the rows. Taking your first column of units, pin one of the four vertical sashing strips (cut in step 3 of "cutting") to the righthand, long side, and stitch, being careful not to stretch the fabric. Press the seams towards the sashing (diagram 3). Repeat with three more rows. You will have one row left over.

diagram 3

NOTE

Pin the columns together carefully and mark the position of the horizontal seams on the wrong side of the sashing before stitching. The fabric can stretch and it is important to get the horizontal rows to line up as you stitch the vertical sashing strips in position. (They have a tendency to creep when being stitched together!)

7 Stitch the spare column of units to the righthand side of the patchwork panel.

ADDING THE BORDERS

1 Pin and stitch one of the four 2 in/5 cm inner border strips (cut in step 3 of "cutting") to one side of the patchwork top. Repeat on the other side. Trim even, then add a strip to the top and bottom. Press and trim.

2 For the middle border, measure the pieced top through the center from side to side. Then join strips to this measurement from the middle border fabric and stitch to the top of the patchwork. Repeat for the bottom strip.

3 Measure the pieced top through the center from top to bottom; then join strips to this measurement from the middle border fabric and stitch to the side of the patchwork. Repeat for the other side.

4 Repeat the measuring and joining for the outer border and attach to all four sides of the quilt. Press your work.

FINISHING

1 Spread the backing right side down on a flat surface, then smooth the batting and the patchwork top, right side up, on top. Fasten together with safety pins or baste in a grid.

2 Machine quilt with a straight stitch, using a walking foot and variegated thread, down each side of the sashing and one side of the outer border.

3 Join the binding strips cut in step 4 of "Cutting" with diagonal seams to make a continuous length to fit all around the quilt. Use to bind the edges with a double-fold binding, mitered at the corners.

Red and White

Designed by Dorothy Wood

The two patterned fabrics used here are part of a range of matching fabrics that give the quilt a 1950s retro look. The circle pattern squares are cut on the straight grain so that the seams are easy to stitch and don't stretch out of shape. The wide binding is made by folding over the extra-large backing fabric, which is a quick and easy way to finish off the edges.

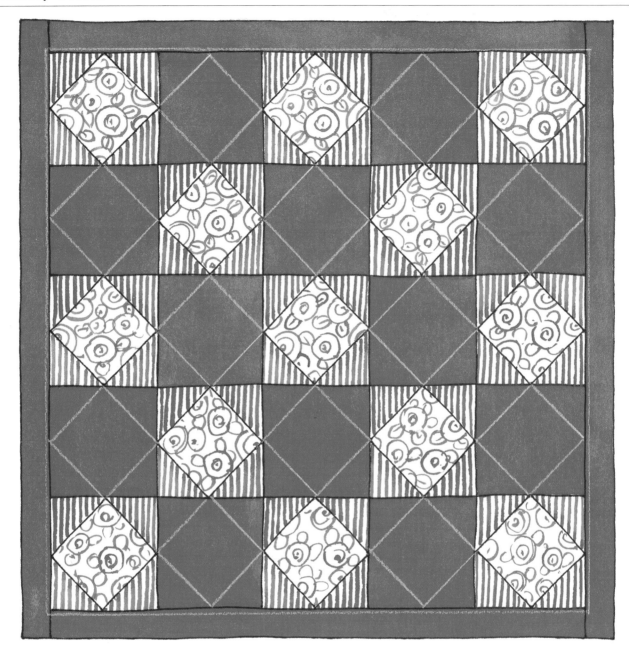

Finished size: 40 x 40 in/102 x 102 cm

MATERIALS
All fabrics used in the quilt top are 45 in/115 cm
wide, 100% cotton.
The backing fabric used is 59 in/150 cm wide.

Red and white circle print: 12 in/30 cm
Red and white stripe: 20 in/51 cm
Solid red: 24 in/60 cm
Backing: red, 50 x 50 in/127 x 127 cm
Batting: 40 x 40 in/102 x 102 cm
White sewing thread
Water soluble pen

ALTERNATIVE COLOR SCHEMES

1 The matching stripe and check patterned fabrics make a subtle combination that can be softened with off-white or brightened up with dark blue; 2 Choose baby pinks, blues and yellow to make a pretty cot quilt. Choose a baby print and pick out some solid colors to coordinate; 3 Contrasting fabrics made from the same print block are ideal for this quilt design. Choose one of the common colors for the whole squares; 4 Spot fabrics are always fun and often found in a range of different colorways that can be mixed and matched.

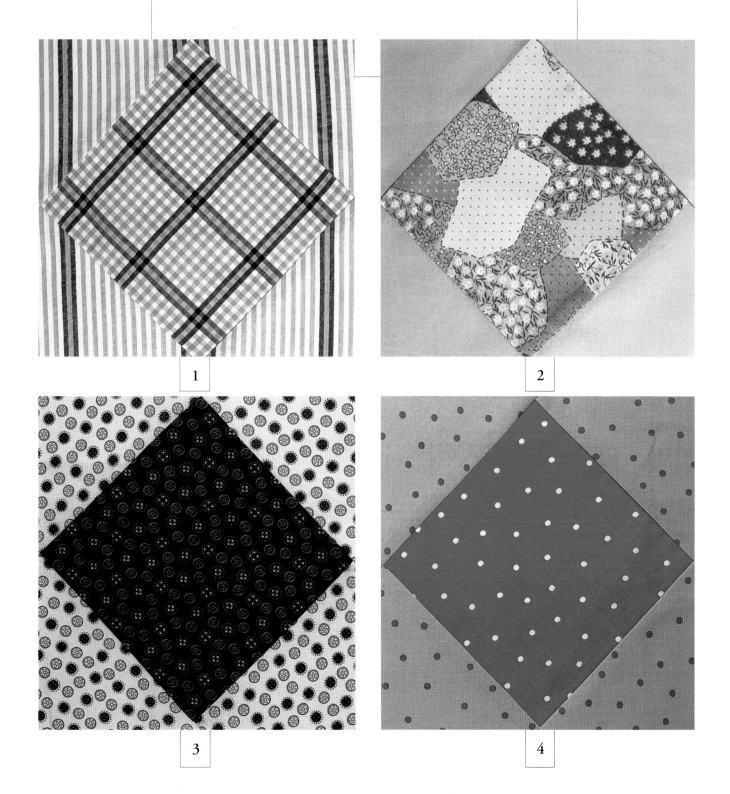

1

2

3

4

CUTTING

1 From the red and white circle print, cut two strips across the width, 6 in/15 cm deep, and cross-cut into thirteen 6 in/15 cm squares. Although they are set as diamonds on the quilt top, cut the squares on the straight grain.

NOTE Take care when cutting the stripes that each square is exactly the same, with the same width of stripe down each side. To make all the striped squares the same, you may need to cut off a narrow strip before cutting the next square.

2 From the red and white stripe, cut three or four strips across the width, 4¾ in/12 cm deep, then cross-cut into twenty-six 4¾ in/12 cm squares. Cut half the squares diagonally from top left to bottom right, and the other half from top right to bottom left.

3 From the red fabric, cut three strips across the width, 8 in/20 cm deep, then cross-cut into twelve 8 in/20 cm squares.

STITCHING

1 Arrange the first block of red circle square and striped triangles so that the stripes run vertically (diagram 1).

diagram 1

2 Lay one of the triangles face down on the square and pin so that an equal amount overhangs at each end. Stitch with a ¼ in/0.75 cm seam (diagram 2). Stitch the same triangle to all the red circle squares. Press the seams towards the striped fabric.

diagram 2

3 Pin and stitch a triangle to the opposite side of each square. Press the seams towards the striped fabric. Pin and stitch the remaining striped triangles to the opposite sides of the squares, so that all the stripes are vertical. Press the seams towards the striped fabric.

4 Following the quilt assembly diagram on page 112, arranging the patchwork blocks alternately with the solid red squares. Pin and stitch the blocks together in rows. Press the seams in adjacent rows in opposite directions.

5 Pin the rows together, matching the seams carefully, and stitch with a ¼ in/0.75 cm seam. Press the seams downwards.

ASSEMBLING

1 Place the backing fabric on a flat surface right side down and smooth out the batting on top. Give the pieced top a final press and lay it on top of the batting right side up, so that there is a 5 in/13 cm border of backing fabric and approximately 3 in/7.5 cm of batting all around. Fasten together with safety pins or baste in a grid.

2 Using the water soluble pen and a quilter's rule, draw lines between the red circle diamonds to mark a similar diamond on the red squares. On the red squares at the edge of the quilt, mark the center point $\frac{1}{4}$ in/0.75 cm from the raw edge before completing the diamond (diagram 3).

diagram 3

3 Thread the machine with white thread. Stitch along the edge of the red circle squares and along all the marked lines in one direction. Turn the quilt and complete the stitching in the other direction. Bring all the thread ends to the right side. At the edge of the quilt, the threads will be tucked behind the binding. Stitch any other thread ends into the quilt.

NOTE When machine quilting, do not stitch beyond the edge on the diamonds at the edge of the quilt because the stitching will be visible on the reverse side.

4 Tuck the cutting mat between the batting and the backing fabric down one side. Using the rotary cutter and quilter's rule, trim the batting to 2 in/5 cm from the edge of the diamonds. Trim all edges the same.

5 Fold the red backing fabric over to the front even with the batting and turn under the edge, so that it butts against the edge of the diamonds. Pin and tack (diagram 4). Fold over and tack the opposite side in the same way.

diagram 4

6 Fold in the two remaining sides to complete the binding. It may be easier to trim some of the excess fabric at the corners to reduce bulk. Slip-stitch the corners only.

7 Machine stitch along the edge of the binding with white thread. Remove all tacking and press the binding lightly. Spray or sponge the quilt top with water to remove the marked lines and hang the quilt to dry.

Star Banner Wallhanging

Designed by Katharine Guerrier

Brighten a dark corner in the house with this vibrant wallhanging. The "Friendship Star" block is quick to make with speed piecing techniques. Setting the blocks on a tilt gives them a contemporary look. An ingenious method of finishing the edges means that there is no binding, saving even more time. Small quilts like this can also be used to display a collection of brooches, badges or even a button collection.

Finished size: 39 x 15 in/99 x 38 cm

MATERIALS

All fabrics used in the patchwork top are
45 in/115 cm wide, 100 cotton.

Turquoise, blue and red: one fat quarter of each
Purple: 20 in/50 cm
Backing: 18 x 42 in/46 x 107 cm
Batting: 18 x 42 in/46 x 107 cm
Tracing paper: one 8½ in/22 cm square
Flat-headed pins
Variegated machine embroidery thread for quilting

ALTERNATIVE COLOR SCHEMES

1 Accentuate the star shapes with a bold fabric set in a neutral background;
2 Soft pastels make a pretty wallhanging for a guest bedroom; 3 Use novelty
fabrics to make a fun wallhanging; 4 These soft lilacs are a soothing combination for a bedroom wall.

1

2

3

4

CUTTING

1 From the four colored fabrics cut $2\frac{7}{8}$ in/7.5 cm squares in the following quantities and colors:
eight red;
six blue;
eight turquoise;
six purple;

then cut $2\frac{1}{2}$ in/6.5 cm squares in the following quantities and colors:
four purple;
five turquoise;
five red;
one blue.

2 From the red, blue and turquoise, cut strips, $2\frac{1}{2}$ in/6.5 cm wide in the following lengths: two $6\frac{1}{2}$ in/16.5 cm and two $10\frac{1}{2}$ in/25.5 cm in each color.

3 From the purple, cut four 4 in/10 cm strips for the borders in the following lengths: two 33 in/84 cm and two 16 in/40.5 cm. Cut one piece, 8 x 17 in/ 20 x 42 cm for the hanging sleeve.

STITCHING

1 Take one red and one purple $2\frac{7}{8}$ in/7.5 cm square and place right sides together. Draw a diagonal line on the reverse of the top square; then stitch down both sides of the line; $\frac{1}{4}$ in/0.75 cm away from it. Cut along the diagonal line and open out to make two half-square triangle units (see diagram 3, page 84). Repeat with the remaining $2\frac{7}{8}$ in/7.5 cm squares to make the following color combinations and in the quantities given:
red/purple: four;
red/blue: eight;
blue/turquoise: four;
turquoise/purple: eight;
red/turquoise: four.

2 Now using four half-square triangle units and five squares for each block make three "Friendship Star" blocks as shown in diagram 1. Use the quilt assembly diagram on page 118 as a guide for the correct color combinations and orientation of seams.

diagram 1

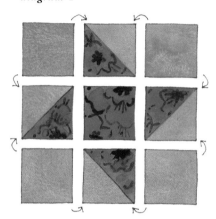

3 Using the $2\frac{1}{2}$ in/6.5 cm-wide strips stitch borders around each of the blocks in the correct color combinations (diagram 2). Press the seams towards the borders.

diagram 2

4 Cut a tracing paper template 8½ in/21.5 cm square. Lay this on each of the blocks in turn, setting the paper at a tilt. Attach the paper to the block with flat-headed pins and cut around the paper (diagram 3). Tilt the two blocks to the left and one to the right.

diagram 3

5 To make the sawtooth borders, stitch the remaining half-square triangle units into four strips of four squares in the following color combinations: red/purple, red/blue, blue/turquoise and turquoise/purple (diagram 4). Press the seams towards the darker fabrics.

diagram 4

6 Following the quilt assembly diagram, stitch the sawtooth borders and blocks together, using the usual seam allowance.

ADDING THE BORDERS

1 Stitch the two longer purple 4 in/10 cm border strips to each side of the pieced top. Then stitch the two shorter ones to the top and bottom, trimming the border strips to length if necessary. Shape the bottom of the quilt by drawing a line from the center point of the bottom border to ½ in/1.5 cm below the seam line at both sides (diagram 5).

diagram 5

FINISHING

1 Cut the backing into two pieces across the width. Then place these two pieces right sides together and stitch along one short edge using a ¼ in/0.75 cm seam but leaving a 6 in/15 cm gap in the center of the seam. Press the seam to one side.

2 Place the pieced top and the backing right sides together and smooth the two layers; then tack together. Trim the backing to the exact size of the quilt.

3 Place the batting on a flat surface and lay the quilt and backing on top with the wrong side of the quilt against the batting. Pin the layers together on the backing side.

4 With the backing on top and the batting underneath, stitch all around the outer edges through all three layers with a walking foot, using a ¼ in/0.75 cm seam allowance. Trim the batting close to the stitching and clip the corners to reduce bulk.

5 Turn the quilt to the right side through the gap in the backing. This will bring the batting between the quilt top and the backing. Finger press the seam flat so that it will lie along the outer edge of the quilt. Smooth the layers out from the center and hold the layers together with a few pins.

6 Machine quilt using a walking foot. Using the variegated machine embroidery thread, outline the block seams and fill in the spaces with zigzag lines. Outline the seams joining the sawtooth borders and the border seams (see page 18).

7 Make a hanging sleeve (see page 18) and attach.

Starry, Starry Lap Quilt

Designed by Rita Whitehorn

A cheerful lap quilt to warm up winter evenings. The simple white patches in between the pieced blocks are embellished with star quilted patterns to echo the bright star fabric used in the border and strip patches.

Finished size: 57 x 46 in/ 145 x 117 cm

MATERIALS

All fabrics used in the patchwork top are
45 in/115 cm wide, 100% cotton.

For the stripes: ¼ yd/25 cm of three plain colors
(mauve, pink and green); ½ yd/50 cm of one
cooler color (turquoise); ½ yd/50 cm of one stronger
color (red)

Star fabric: 2 yds/2 m
White: ½ yd/50 cm
Backing: 1¾ yds/1.6 m
Batting: 100% cotton, 60 x 50 in/130 x 155 cm
Template plastic
Marking pencil
Quilting threads: various colors to match the stripes

ALTERNATIVE COLOR SCHEMES

In each of these different colorways the colors of the plain blocks have been picked out and repeated in the strips: 1 Choosing a striped fabric for the plain blocks makes a visually bold quilt; 2 Blues and aquas make a fresh, crisp color combination for a country-style bedroom; 3 The clear blue print leads the way to a sunny color scheme; 4 A glowing color scheme based on the glittering insect print.

1

2

3

4

CUTTING

1 From each of the five colors for the stripes and from the star fabric, cut two strips, 2¼ in/5.5 cm deep, across the width of the fabric.

2 From the white fabric, cut six squares, 10½ in/26.5 cm wide.

3 From the turquoise, cut four strips, 2½ in/6 cm deep, across the width for the inner border.

4 From the red fabric, cut four strips 1½ in/4 cm deep, across the width for the middle border. The remainder will be cut later for the binding.

5 From the star fabric, cut four strips, 5½ in/14 cm deep, across the width for the outer border.

STITCHING

1 Lay out one of each of the 2¼ in/5.5 cm-wide strips in your chosen sequence; then stitch together using a ¼ in/0.75 cm seam allowance and press towards the darker fabrics (diagram 1).

diagram 1

2 Repeat step one above to make another block of stripes.

3 Sub-cut the above sections into six 10½ in/26.5 cm blocks (diagram 2).

diagram 2

4 Following the quilt assembly diagram on page 124, lay out the striped and white squares in three columns, four squares deep.

5 To assemble the first row, stitch a striped block to a white block, using the usual seam allowance; then stitch another striped block to the other side of the white block. Press the seams towards the striped blocks.

6 To assemble the second row, stitch a white block to a striped block; then stitch a second white block to the other side of the striped block.

7 Pin and stitch the first row to the second row, being careful to match seams (diagram 3).

diagram 3

8 Stitch the third row like the first and the fourth row like the second. Pin and stitch these two rows together.

9 Finally, pin and stitch the unit made in step 7 to the unit made in step 8. Press the seams all in the same direction.

ADDING THE BORDERS

1 To make the inner border, stitch one turquoise 2½ in/6 cm strip to the top and one to the bottom of the pieced top, pressing seams towards the border. Trim the excess fabric; then stitch the remaining turquoise strips on to both sides and press as before.

2 To make the middle border, stitch one red 1½ in/4 cm strip to the top and one to the bottom of the pieced top, pressing seams towards the border. Trim the excess fabric; then stitch the remaining red strips on to both sides and press as before.

3 To make the outer border, stitch one 5½ in/14 cm star strip to the top and one to the bottom of the patchwork top, pressing seams towards the border. Trim the excess fabric, then stitch on the remaining star strips to both side borders and press as before.

FINISHING

1 Make a star template from the template plastic in both of the sizes given opposite. Place these randomly on the white squares of the patchwork top and draw around the shape lightly with the marking pencil.

2 Spread the backing right side down on a flat surface, then smooth the batting and the pieced top, right side up, on top. Fasten together with safety pins or baste in a grid.

3 Hand quilt around the marked stars using different colors of quilting thread.

4 Machine or hand quilt in-the-ditch between the middle and outer borders and between the stripes as shown in diagram 4.

diagram 4

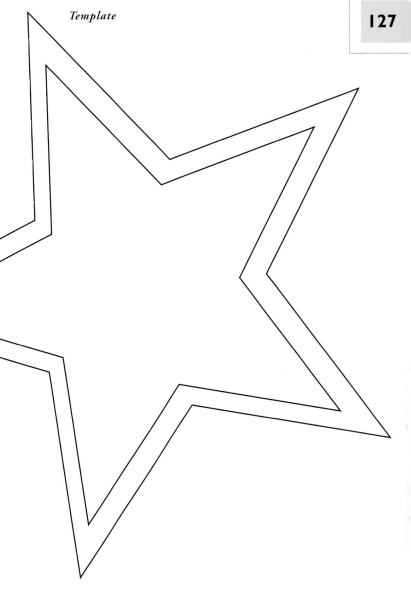

Template

5 Trim off any excess batting and backing fabric even with the pieced top.

6 Measure the quilt through the center from top to bottom and cut two 2½ in/6 cm-wide binding strips to this length. Fold one binding strip in half length-wise, wrong sides together, and pin to the side of the quilt, matching raw edges. Stitch approximately ½ in/1.5 cm in from the edge. Fold over to the back of the quilt and slip-stitch down. Do the same on the opposite side of the quilt with the remaining strip.

7 Measure the quilt through the center from side to side and add 1½ in/4 cm to this for turning. Cut two more 2½ in/6 cm-wide binding strips to this length, joining if necessary. Fold in half as before. Pin and stitch to the top and bottom of the quilt, turning in a short hem at either end before folding to the back.

Blue Ribbon Throw

Designed by Sharon Chambers

Impress your friends with the woven effect of blue ribbons in this intricate-looking but simply pieced throw, backed with a sunny yellow. If you're hoping for a fast finish, this one's a sure bet, and it can easily be made bigger for a bed quilt by adding more blocks.

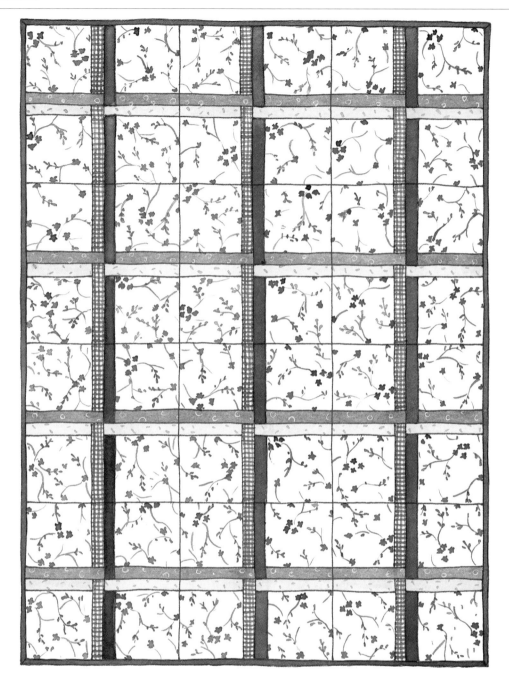

Finished size: 54 x 42 in/140 x 105 cm

MATERIALS
All fabrics used in the quilt top are 45 in/115 cm wide, 100% cotton.

For the background: blue and white all-over floral patterned fabric, $1\frac{2}{3}$ yds/1.5 m
For the ribbons: four contrasting blue fabrics, a long $\frac{1}{4}$ yd/25 cm of each
Backing: yellow, $1\frac{5}{8}$ yds/1.5 m
Binding: dark blue, $\frac{5}{8}$ yd/50 cm
Batting: 46 x 58 in/115 x 150 cm
Machine quilting thread

NOTE
These fabrics need to be easily distinguished from each other, as well as from the background. I chose a dark blue tone-on-tone abstract, a medium/dark geometric, a medium blue and white check and a light/medium small floral print, all of which look different from each other and stand out well against the light floral background.

ALTERNATIVE COLOR SCHEMES

1 You can give this quilt a fresh look by putting the blue ribbons on a soft yellow background; 2 A pale peach background makes a very pretty color combination; 3 A rose-colored ground is also soft and cottagey; 4 For those who prefer a brighter look, try weaving the blue ribbons across a rich fuchsia abstract print.

CUTTING

1 From the floral patterned background fabric, cut eight strips, 6½ in/16.5 cm deep, across the width of the fabric. Trim the selvages off. Cross-cut each strip into six squares 6½ x 6½ in/16.5 x 16.5 cm.

2 From one of the ribbon fabrics, cut one strip, 7½ in/19 cm deep, across the width of the fabric. Trim the selvages off. Starting at one end, cross-cut the strip into 12 rectangles 1½ in/4 cm wide. Set these aside. Reduce the depth of the remaining strip, making it 6½ in/16.5 cm deep. From this, cross-cut 12 more rectangles 1½ in/4 cm wide (diagram 1). Set aside.

diagram 1

3 Repeat step 2 for the remaining three ribbon fabrics.

4 From the binding fabric, cut six strips, 2½ in/6.5 cm deep, across the width of the fabric.

STITCHING

There are 12 blocks altogether. They are all the same pattern, and they are all stitched exactly the same, but with four different pairings of the ribbon fabrics. All seams are stitched with a ¼ in/0.75 cm seam allowance.

1 Study diagram 2 which shows the four block combinations. Organize your strips to match. In Group A place the **short** medium blue and white check strips and the **long** medium/dark geometric strips. In Group B place the **short** medium/dark geometric strips and the **long** dark tone-on-tone strips. In Group C place the **short** light/medium small floral strips and the **long**

medium blue and white check strips. In Group D place the **short** dark tone-on-tone strips and the **long** light/medium small floral strips. You will be stitching all 12 blocks in one group at the same time, chain-piecing for efficiency.

diagram 2

NOTE Stitching all of the blocks in a group at the same time saves confusion and means there is less risk of making a mistake.

2 Place 12 of the background squares and all of the strips from Group A next to your machine. With right sides together, stitch a short strip to one side of a center square. Without breaking the thread, stitch the second short strip and another square together. Continue until all 12 are stitched. Cut them apart and press all seams towards the short strip.

3 Stack all the partially-stitched blocks right side up next to your machine with the just-stitched strip at the top so that they are correctly aligned for adding the next strip. Stitch a long strip to the righthand side of the partially-stitched block and, without breaking the thread, do the same for the other 11 blocks in that group. Clip the threads and press the seams towards the long strip.

4 Repeat steps 2 and 3 for groups B, C and D. Pin an identifying letter to each finished stack if it helps to keep them organized.

5 Following diagram 2, lay your stacks in similar positions. Stitch all of the A units to the Bs and all of the C units to the Ds (diagram 3). Press the seams towards the Bs and the Cs.

diagram 3

6 Pin and stitch the two halves together to make 12 larger blocks (diagram 4).

diagram 4

7 Following the quilt assembly diagram on page 130, lay out the blocks in sequence. Pin and stitch these together into four rows of three units each. Stitch the rows together. Make sure all the blocks stay in the correct alignment, and carefully match all seam lines, pinning as necessary. Press the last seams towards the bottom of the quilt.

FINISHING

1 Measure the pieced top and cut the batting and the backing fabric at least 1 in/2.5 cm larger all around.

2 Spread the backing right side down on a flat surface; then smooth the batting and the patchwork top, right side up, on top. Fasten together with safety pins.

3 Using a walking foot, machine quilt through all three layers along the seam lines.

4 Join the binding strips into one long length. Press in half, wrong sides together, down the entire length. Use to bind the quilt with a double-fold binding, mitered at the corners.

Chenille Hearts

Designed by Sarah Wellfair

The chenille technique, also known as "slashing," is a great way to use up all those ugly fabrics from your stash – when they're used for the lower layers, they don't show, but they add to the felted edges when they've been cut and washed. This technique makes quite a heavy quilt because it's made up of four layers, but it is very soft and cozy.

Finished size: 37¾ x 34½ in/96.5 x 85.5 cm

MATERIALS

All fabrics used in the quilt top are 45 in/115 cm wide, 100% cotton.

Layers: plain purple, 2⅛ yds/2 m and bright pink, 1⅓ yds/1 m

Background: patterned purple, 1⅓ yds/1 m

Hearts: yellow and green, 10 in/25 cm of each

Backing: dark purple, 1⅓ yds/1 m

Lightweight card or plastic for template (optional)

Spray basting glue

Long ruler and marking pencil

Machine sewing cotton: 3 reels of thread to match backing

Chenille or slash cutter or sharp embroidery scissors

Binding: yellow, 12 in/30 cm

ALTERNATIVE COLOR SCHEMES

1 The use of the batik stripe as the background fabric gives a bright orange in the slashes, contrasting with the blue and green hearts; 2 This range of Christmas fabrics on a cream and gold background makes a striking festive throw; 3 This design uses just two colorways from the same fabric design, creating a subtle contrast; 4 Setting the bright colors of the hearts against a calico background accentuates the heart motif.

1

2

3

4

CUTTING

1 From the plain purple, cut two pieces,
37 x 42 in/94 x 106.5 cm, and from the pink layer
fabric, cut one piece of the same size.

2 Cut the purple patterned background fabric as the
same size as the plain fabrics.

3 Enlarge the heart motif opposite, then cut out the
shape in card or plastic and use it to cut four hearts
out of each of the three bright fabrics (pink, yellow
and green), making sure they are on the straight
grain.

STITCHING

1 Press the dark purple backing, and lay right sides
down on the work surface.

2 Lay the three plain fabric pieces right sides up
with the pink in the middle. Then lay the purple
patterned background fabric on top, right side up,
and baste in place.

3 Place the four fabric sandwiches on top of the
backing fabric. These should be at least 1 in/2.5 cm
smaller all around than the backing. Spray glue baste
or tack these in place. Your stack of fabrics should be
five deep (diagram 1).

diagram 1

4 Following diagram 2 below for positioning, spray
glue baste or tack the hearts on top of the patterned
purple, making sure they are on the straight grain.

5 Using a long ruler and pencil draw a line across
the quilt at a 45 degree angle, starting in the bottom
righthand corner. This is your first stitching line.

6 It is a good idea to stitch using a walking foot if
you have one. Stitch on the line. Then, without breaking the thread, turn the quilt and stitch another line
exactly parallel to the first, $\frac{1}{4}$ in/0.75 cm away from
it. Repeat at the other end and continue until you
reach the edge of the quilt (diagram 2). Turn the quilt
and stitch the remaining half in the same way, so that
the quilt is now covered with a grid of diagonal
stitched lines.

diagram 2

7 Using sharp embroidery scissors, cut the top four fabrics between the diagonal lines of stitching for 1 in/2.5 cm, being careful not to cut the backing fabric. Do this at the start of every channel between the stitched lines. This will help when slashing (diagram 3).

diagram 3

Template
Enlarge by 200%

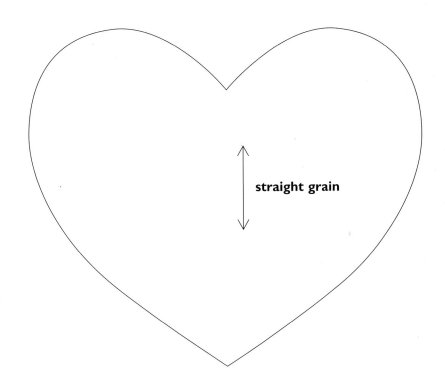

straight grain

8 Insert your slash cutter or very sharp scissors between the rows of stitching on the sides you have just cut. Carefully slash the fabric all the way along the channels, again being careful not to cut the backing. Slash all the channels. Take out any tacking.

9 Now that you have slashed your fabric, you will need to wash it in a washing machine to make the chenille bloom and fluff. A cool wash is usually suitable for most fabrics. Tumble-dry the quilt if possible.

10 Because you have stitched and cut on the bias, your work may be a little out of shape after washing. Square it up using a rotary cutter and cutting mat, trimming off the excess backing fabric at the same time.

11 Measure the quilt through the center from top to bottom and cut two 3 in/7.5 cm-wide binding strips to this length. Fold one binding strip in half lengthwise, wrong sides together, and pin to the side of the

quilt, matching raw edges. Stitch approximately
½ in/1.5 cm in from the edge. Fold over to the back
of the quilt and slip-stitch down. Do the same on the
opposite side of the quilt with the remaining strip.

13 Measure the quilt through the center from side to
side and add 1½ in/4 cm to this for turning. Cut two
more 3 in/7.5 cm-wide binding strips to this length.
Stitch to the top and bottom of the quilt as before,
turning in a short hem at either end before folding to
the back.

NOTE A chenille quilt does not need to
be quilted.

THE CONTRIBUTORS

Sharon Chambers divides her time between teaching quilt techniques, quilt designing and working at The Quilt Room in Dorking, Surrey, England.

Nikki Foley has a degree in interior design and uses this to her advantage when designing quilts and patterns for her business "The Sewing Shed." Also, as a qualified adult education teacher she lets others share in her creativity in the workshops she runs. Further information is available by contacting her at thesewingshed@aol.com

Katharine Guerrier is a leading quilt designer who frequently exhibits in national shows. She is also author of a number of books on quilt techniques.

Jean Hunt is an experienced teacher, having taught patchwork for many years in her home-town of Stroud, Gloucestershire, England. She is the resident teacher for Abigail Crafts, based in Stonehouse, leading a group of 50 pupils, called the "Hunt Stitchers."

Gail Smith opened a patchwork shop after completing a City and Guild course; she is a qualified adult education teacher, running local patchwork groups, and designing quilt kits and other items to sell in her shop, "Abigail Crafts." There is also a website: www.abigailcrafts.co.uk, featuring fabrics similar to those used in her Matrix Quilt.

Sarah Wellfair is a qualified teacher who runs a full program of workshops from her patchwork shop, Goose Chase Quilting, at Leckhampton in Gloucestershire, England. She also produces a range of quilt patterns available from the shop.

Rita Whitehorn is an experienced quiltmaker and designer who makes quilts by commission. She particularly enjoys making scrap quilts.

Alison Wood started making quilts a little over 10 years ago and has become more passionate about the craft with each passing year. She teaches classes and works part-time at The Quilt Room in Dorking, Surrey, England and finds it hugely rewarding to help others develop their skills.

Dorothy Wood is an author and designer who has written and contributed to over 20 needle-craft books. She studied dress and design in Edinburgh before specializing in embroidery and textiles at Goldsmith's College, London.

INDEX